WRITING A TELEVISION PLAY

WRITING A TELEVISION PLAY

By

Michelle Cousin

Publishers　　　THE WRITER, INC.　　　*Boston*

Library of Congress Cataloging in Publication Data

Cousin, Michelle.
   Writing a television play.
   1. Television authorship.   I. Title.
PN1992.7.C6   808.2'2   75-14493
ISBN 0-87116-088-9

MANUFACTURED IN THE UNITED STATES OF AMERICA

To my students

Acknowledgments

To Catherine Blankenship who initiated this project—and to my family and friends who encouraged the writing of this book. A special thanks to Marvin Hammerman, Patricia Rosenthal, Ruth Miles, Rose Blacker and Francis E. Voermans for their valuable assistance . . .

And to my editor and publisher, Sylvia and Abe Burack, who made the writing of this book a pleasure.

Contents

A Note from the Author

How do you write a teleplay? It's the question uppermost in the minds of my students as we face each other at the beginning of a semester.

There is no simple answer because a teleplay is far from simple. It requires a basic talent plus a keen ear, an observant eye, a compassionate nature, a vivid imagination—and one other essential: the technical know-how, the intelligent use of the tools of the craft. For television writing *is* a craft, and as such, can be taught. The terminology of a teleplay, its specific form on paper, the film techniques, the dramatic structure—all of the elements that constitute a play can be explored step by step, practiced, and finally shaped into a creative work.

Beginning writers, for the most part, have an awareness, a curiosity about the human condition, and a persistent urging that finally impels them to take the first step toward self-expression.

If it were the short story or the novel they were exploring, they would be guided gently to a discovery of their own resources. Craftsmanship, of course, would be discussed, but in an unrestrained atmosphere with no limitation as to time, for in prose writing the subject matter determines the length of the manuscript.

This is not true in television. The creative writer is asked to conform to a rigid discipline governed by the clock. Time is a commodity in television and the subject matter must fill the required blocks of time. To write within its confines, to create a professional piece of work that stimulates and entertains the viewer, necessitates a *harnessing* of creativity. A good television play is compact, finely constructed—a clean entity with no dangling threads.

Is the writing of such a dramatic work an impossible goal for the beginner? On the contrary. It is a challenging, exhilarating experience with its own special bonus. Since most television is on film today, the talented aspirant who masters the technique of writing a teleplay learns much about motion picture technique as well. As a matter of fact, there will be references in this book to movies and stage plays, for once the dramatic structure is understood, one gains a deeper insight into these other forms of writing.

I am assuming that you, the reader, are interested in television writing from the professional standpoint. In earlier years, the market was wide open to new people who could contribute to the insatiable appetite of this growing medium. It would be less than honest to pretend that such is the case today. Commercial television is an industry, a business that must show profit in order for it to exist. Costs have spiraled in the past few years, making many kinds of dramatic shows prohibitively expensive. Trends, too, play an important part in an industry constantly striving to satisfy the public taste.

And yet, if there is one consistent quality about television, it is *change.* Never static, always fluctuating, each new season can bring its own surprises. The mini-series, the after-school specials for children, the ninety-minute daytime dramas are examples of innovative programming that depends on talented free-lancers.

For all its faults, television is still one of the greatest marvels of our age. It can provoke, stimulate, entertain, educate. Occasionally it can capture a vision, illuminate a truth, and in its *intimacy,* it can reflect the moment and nostalgically look back at the past.

As it continues to grow, to change, it will need the new craftsmen who have learned to channel creativity for this specialized profession.

It is my hope that this book will familiarize you with this profession and give you clear, practical, concise information on how to write a teleplay. Granted, you may be hundreds of miles away from the production centers in California and New York. You may not have access to a class in which you can learn your craft. But I like to think that this book will perhaps simulate a classroom experience and help you ultimately to write a television play. Toward this end, I have included in the latter part of the book an actual "diary of a teleplay" in which we trace a half-hour script from its inception to the finished work, pointing out all of the technique explored in the chapters preceding it.

To all of you who watch television and think, "I can do better," good luck—and good writing.

—MICHELLE COUSIN

Part One
EXPLORATION

I
THE NATURE OF TELEVISION FILM

THE NEXT time you watch a television play, look at the screen critically, analytically. This is not easy, I know, especially if it's an absorbing drama that quickly involves the viewer. But as a beginning writer, you want more than involvement. You want technical knowledge. For you, the television screen is a learning device which you can use to study the intricate details of this exciting medium. As you watch the drama on the screen before you, become aware of the various elements: the sets, the lighting, the music to heighten the action. Count the *change* of sets—the interiors, the exteriors. And follow the camera as it plays on the faces of the people talking. First, perhaps, only the face of the man fills the screen; then the face of the woman. Again the camera shifts, this time to include both of them as they continue talking.

As part of the viewing audience, you were probably unaware of these changes, for your eyes accommodated to them as easily as blinking. But as a writer, you must recognize this fluidity, for it marks one of the essential differences between the film and any of the related arts (live television, legitimate theatre).

In contrast to a *moving* picture, a theatrical play within the boundaries of a proscenium arch is very limited. Not that it lacks drama. In a good play, the action comes from the inner conflict of the characters, and even a one-set play can be extremely *moving*

3

from an emotional standpoint. But from a technical viewpoint, the author is bound to a designated area.

Similarly, the live shows in the early days of television had certain technical limitations. Though the camera gave the drama an added dimension, the writer was still confined to a few sets, all interiors. His cast was, of necessity, small. And he had the added burden of planning adequate time for an actor to change his costume and get to another set for the following scene. Despite these conditions, however, the writer, much like his counterpart in the theatre, experienced a sense of *oneness* as he watched his play take shape. Starting from the beginning, he followed its evolvement scene by scene to the end of the play. As rehearsals went on, a strong bond usually developed among writer, director, cast and crew. They were an entity and their highly concentrated work in a short time span resulted in a live performance that had all the electric quality of an opening night on Broadway.

From live shows to film

What a contrast to the creation of a film! Today a teleplay is the sum of the talents of many different craftsmen who put a picture together piece by piece like a jigsaw puzzle. There is seldom any logical sequence in the making of a picture. At the discretion of the director, the last scene could be filmed first. Certainly the location scenes (let's assume the script calls for a ski resort) are all shot within one concentrated period of time. Budget is the primary factor here. A great deal of money can be saved by transporting all the equipment, actors, and crew to the location at the same time. All the ski scenes, though they are interspersed throughout the script, are filmed within this period. Since the shots are numbered, the editor can easily fit them into their proper sequence.

It is interesting to realize that the audience totally accepts what it sees and is unaware of the intricate tricks of the film-maker. I was one of this vast audience years ago before I made the transition from live television writing to film. I remember seeing a movie in which I recognized my college campus. Fascinated, I watched the actress walk up the familiar path to the ivy-covered building that housed the Drama Department I knew so well. I was astonished when the actress opened the door and stepped into an elegant reception hall complete with thick carpeting, a winding staircase, and a magnificent chandelier. It was a far cry from the peeling plaster and the ugly light fixture that was there when I went to school. "Wouldn't you know," I thought wryly, "they wait for me to graduate and then remodel the place."

You can imagine my surprise when, a year later, I visited the campus, walked up the path leading to the same building, opened the door to what I thought was the new reception hall—only to discover the same peeling plaster and the ugly light fixture of my college days.

It was a weird moment. I went back in my mind to the movie. I distinctly saw the actress open the door and enter a luxurious hall. What I had to realize was that the exterior scene (the campus) ended the moment the actress put her hand on the doorknob. The interior scene (the hall) was an entirely different set and could have been filmed miles away and weeks before the preceding scene. Its number designated it to be placed directly after the campus scene, so in the completed picture it *looked* as if the actress had opened the door and stepped into the hall. Only then did it become a part of the natural continuity of the picture. In the formative stages these two scenes, like all the other scenes, were actually "bits and pieces" of the film as a whole.

Fragments into a creative whole

A new writer is easily disturbed by this jigsaw element, but the confusion is due to an ignorance of the nature of film. Once he accepts the magic, the ingenious tricks of the trade, he experiences a creative freedom he never dreamed possible. His sets can be anywhere from Kalamazoo to Marrakech. He can go from a plane to a train to a car speeding along the highway. From a coal miner's hut to a fantasy castle, there is nothing he can imagine that cannot be realized on screen. As for the characters in a film, depending upon the budget, the writer can ask for as many actors as the script requires. Since the scenes are shot in fragments, he needn't worry about costume changes and adequate time for actors to get from one set to another. As a matter of fact, he needn't worry about the technical end at all. He has only to dream the dream and translate it properly into script form for the other craftsmen.

"But," you may ask, "how can you dream in fragments? If the nature of film is bits and pieces, how can a writer achieve any sense of wholeness—of continuity?"

The fact is, the writer *can* and *must* achieve this wholeness. From the moment he is sparked by an idea to the subsequent working out of the plot, characters, and theme, the writer must see his play as an entity and write it that way in logical progression. *Only he has this privilege.* Once the script is written, it will be broken into segments by the director, set designer, and others. And when all the segments are filmed, they will be put together by the editor to emerge on the screen as a whole—as the writer conceived it.

For this to happen, however, the writer requires a special skill in order to communicate with the other craftsmen. He should have a peripheral knowledge at least of how film is made, and as a professional writer, he should know the correct form, the proper terminology of a written teleplay or film script.

In the following chapters, we will learn not only this form, but the elements of dramatic construction that constitute a television play.

II

THE BASIC TOOLS

EVERY PROFESSION has its terminology—its unique vocabulary. Television is no exception. The technical words are important and equally important is *how* they are placed on the page. The spacing, the margins, upper and lower case letters, all the minute details mark the professional tone of the writer. Conversely, a sloppy script—one that doesn't adhere to form—makes a negative impression and brands the writer an amateur even before the work is read.

Some aspiring TV scriptwriters think this is unjust. They claim the "play's the thing," and they don't see why they have to bother with the technicalities. I ask them to consider this: Producers, editors and agents are not in the business of teaching. They may be looking for talent but they want that talent on a professional level. In this highly pressured field, there is no time for them to nurture a beginner. One glance at the first page of your script will tell them whether or not you know your craft. Even the *weight* of your script will give them an indication. It sounds ludicrous, but when I was editing a half-hour live television show years ago, the producer told me to hold the manuscript and feel the weight of it. If it was very light (about ten or twelve pages), I could save myself the trouble of reading it, for the writer had written an anecdote, not a play. If it was extremely heavy (about ninety pages), it was obviously not a half-hour show and would not do for our program. A live half-hour show constituted about twenty-eight pages (a little more or less didn't matter), and only a manuscript that answered that requisite could be read.

The correct teleplay form on paper, therefore, has a direct bearing on the number of pages produced which, in turn, relates to the proper timing. Time is a vital concern in the television industry. A writer must always be aware of the clock. Granted, there is a flexibility in the filming of the teleplay and cuts can be made to accommodate the clock. But in general, the writer should be aware of the limitations:

half-hour teleplay	about 28–32 pages
hour teleplay	about 65–70 pages
hour and a half teleplay	about 105–110 pages

Before we examine the basic camera terminology, it's important to remember that the writer is asked to use only *minimum* camera directions. In teleplay parlance, he is required to write a *loose* script. This means that only the essential camera technique is needed: the numbering of the shots, the setting of the scenes, the transitions from one scene to the other—these are basic and are necessary to the forward movement of the story. Once the dialogue starts, the writer should not intrude with "calling the shots." This is the director's province. When the script is written and accepted, a *tight shooting script* will be made, at which time the writer may, or may not, be called to designate every shot. It is usually the director who works on this project, for it is his artistry that will translate the script to the screen. For all practical purposes, in teleplays and film, loose scripts are preferred for first readings. An editor or producer looks for the "wholeness" we mentioned before. He wants to get the feel of the story, the depth of the characters, the theme, the plot. A tight script with all the technical directions is too difficult to follow and intrudes into the dramatic structure.

Technical terms

A knowledge of the following terms will be more than adequate for the purpose of writing a teleplay:

FADE IN—These are the first words of any script. It means that the screen is dark and that it gradually fades into light as the picture appears. It is the opening—a beginning—much like the curtain rising on stage.

FADE OUT—The screen gradually goes to black as the picture literally "fades out" (or away). When used between scenes, it denotes passage of time. If you FADE OUT of one scene, you always FADE IN to the next scene, for when the screen is black, it must gradually become light again. FADE OUT is used at the end of the play as a "closing curtain."

DISSOLVE—This too is a transition—a bridge from one scene to the next. In a DISSOLVE, the screen never goes completely black. Actually, there are *two* pictures on the screen at the same time: the one fading out and the new scene fading in which is superimposed upon the first picture. Gradually the fade-out frame disappears, leaving the new scene to fill up the screen. A DISSOLVE is effective for smooth transitions between scenes denoting a short time lapse. Longer time indications between scenes are more effective with the FADE OUT, FADE IN method.

CUT TO:—This is the most obvious, the most common type of direction to quickly get from one scene to another. When we CUT TO the next scene, there is seldom a time lapse involved. It is a sharp, instantaneous transition. For example, in the scene I described in the previous chapter about the actress walking up the campus path to the door of the building, when she places her hand on the doorknob, we CUT TO the next scene in the hall. It is such a fast cut, however, and it follows so logically in the script, that we don't have to use the words CUT TO in order to indicate the transition. We do, however, number the next shot (as she enters the hall). The number implies CUT TO.

PAN—The word is short for *panorama* which, according to the dictionary, is "a constantly changing scene"; in other words, *movement,* which is the very essence of film. When a character, for example, gets up from a sofa and walks to the window, the camera PANS (or moves with him). This is so elemental in terms of camera direction that the writer need not indicate it. However, suppose you have a courtroom scene and you want to show the faces of the jury as the lawyer is summing up. You indicate this by writing: CAMERA PANS to the faces of the jury as the lawyer speaks.

> LAWYER (voice over)
> Ladies and gentlemen of the
> jury—(etc.)

As the lawyer continues to speak, the camera moves across a group of people. It goes from one face to the other, pausing to give us a close look at the individual expressions. When the camera has completed the PANNING of the jury, we go back to the lawyer.

Inanimate objects are also subjects for PANNING when the objects are important to the script. In mystery dramas, the camera will often PAN to certain things in a room in which the murder has been committed. A book can be significant, a letter-opener on a desk, an open window. . . . These are the details that are pointed up by the PANNING of the camera.

DOLLY IN—a DOLLY is actually a low, flat wheeled frame for supporting heavy objects. In this case, the object is a camera. It's a very *mobile* camera because it can DOLLY IN or MOVE IN on an object or person in order to give us a closer look.

Conversely, DOLLY BACK or PULL BACK means that the camera moves away from an object or person, taking in the setting as it moves back. For example, a scene is opened with a CLOSE SHOT of a clock on a nighttable. As we DOLLY BACK, we see a disheveled bedroom—an empty, unmade single bed—and finally the occupant of the room—a tall, gaunt woman in her fifties who is looking out of the window anxiously. Here, without dialogue, we've established a mood, a set, and a tense situation.

LONG SHOT, MEDIUM SHOT, and CLOSE SHOT are, I think, self-explanatory and we need only touch on them. The LONG SHOT, taken from a distance, gives us a wide sweep of the scene. The MEDIUM SHOT is considerably closer, showing us the actors in finer detail in their setting. The CLOSE SHOT fills the entire screen with an actor's face (or object). It can reveal intense emotion as it focuses on the eyes or the mouth. In REACTION SHOTS, it points up the reaction of a character to what is being said.

POV SHOT simply means POINT OF VIEW. It is used when you want to show what a character is looking at. For example: A woman in her kitchen hears the sound of a violin being played. She leaves the sink and walks to the window. She looks out. The next shot is what she presumably sees from her window:

POV-WOMAN EXT. COURTYARD—DAY

A shabbily-dressed, middle-aged man is playing the violin.

INT. KITCHEN—DAY

The woman opens the window.

Creating a scene

Now that we know the terms, let's create our own scene—the opening scene of a teleplay—and see how it looks on paper in proper teleplay form. We'll use the campus background similar to the one I described in the previous chapter. Basically, we want to establish the conflict between a freshman student, Karen Summers, and the Dean of Women, Dr. Hazel Taylor. At this point, we are not concerned with the plot line or the dialogue. We are merely using the situation to exemplify the typographical appearance of dialogue and directions.

Insert blank paper into your typewriter, set one-inch left-hand margin and indent a half-inch with tabular key. Then type in capital letters, FADE IN, followed by a colon. These are the first two words on any script written for television.

(Example)

    FADE IN:

Leave a double space directly under these words and return to regular left margin and type the *number* that designates the scene outside the margin.

(Example)

1.

Now, on the same line as the number (under FADE IN), we type, in capital letters:

(Example)

1. EXT. CAMPUS—DAY

This line is absolutely essential in a teleplay. It quickly indicates to the various craftsmen vital information about the individual scene. If it is outdoors—a terrace, a mountain-top, a street—it is naturally an EXTERIOR scene. If it is indoors—a living room, an office, a foyer—it is an INTERIOR scene. We use the abbreviations EXT. and INT. in the teleplay form. Next to these words, we indicate the type of location (kitchen, street, terrace, etc.) and after a dash, we write DAY or NIGHT. This is for the lighting man. Nothing else is written on this line. Below this line, there will be ample opportunity to describe the set, the time of day (early morning, dusk, whatever). Let's review what we have so far.

FADE IN:

1. EXT. CAMPUS—DAY

Now, double-space directly below this line. In lower case, starting with a one-and-a half-inch indention (below EXT.) and continuing clear across the page, write in any of the details and directions that are necessary to set your scene. You may take as many lines as you need being careful to *single-space* the lines within this paragraph. Remember that a teleplay is always written in the *present tense*. As you visualize the action, assume that it is happening now—on the screen—in front of you.

Let's go back to the scene and fill in the *directive* paragraph.

```
    FADE IN:

1.  EXT. CAMPUS -- DAY

        LONG SHOT of a section of a typical
        California college campus on a sunny
        Spring afternoon. A few students are
        leisurely strolling up a well-tended
        path that leads to an ivy-covered
        building. DOLLY IN to KAREN SUMMERS
        who is walking quickly, a determined
        look on her young, expressive face.
        KAREN is eighteen, extremely pretty,
        very sure of herself. CAMERA FOLLOWS
        her as she walks to the entrance of
        the building, puts her hand on the
        doorknob, and opens the door.
```

Let's analyze the above paragraph. We open with the LONG SHOT because we want to give the audience an "overall" feeling of where we are. A LONG SHOT of the campus, the students, the ivy-covered building immediately establishes our setting. Once this is done, we focus on our character, KAREN, whom the CAMERA FOLLOWS to the door of the building. Note that we capitalize her name the first time we mention her, and then immediately describe her. This is a rule in teleplay writing. Whenever a character is mentioned for the first time, it is necessary to give a short description so that the reader will visualize the person instantly. We indicate that the camera moves with her in the scene. The writer has the option of writing CAMERA FOLLOWS her (as we did above). It is not imperative. It is usually taken for granted. Note that all camera directions are in capital letters.

To continue the script, we cut to the next scene—double-space directly after the previous paragraph. We do not write CUT TO because, as I pointed out earlier, it is implied. We do, however, *number* our next shot.

To clarify the example, I'll begin with the last part of the previous scene and continue to the next:

```
CAMERA FOLLOWS her as she walks to the
entrance of the building, puts her hand
on the doorknob, and opens the door.

2.   INT. HALL -- DAY

This is the reception area of the
executive offices of the college.  The
building, which was once a chateau,
retains its old-fashioned charm.  The
hall is large, impressive, thickly
carpeted and beautifully appointed
with its crystal chandelier and
graceful winding staircase.  Karen
```

```
        enters and is about to walk up the
        steps when she sees DR. HAZEL TAYLOR,
        the Dean of Women, at the top of the
        landing.  DR. TAYLOR is fiftyish,
        distinguished, inclined to look stern.
        Karen waits as Dr. Taylor walks down
        the steps.
```

I assume, by now, the format of above scene is self-explanatory. Note that we described the set as well as the new character, Dr. Taylor. We had no camera directions at all in this scene. Again, let me emphasize the need in a loose teleplay to keep directions to a minimum.

Our next step is *dialogue* and how to indicate the speeches properly in teleplay form. In the middle of the page, double-space after the previous paragraph, type in the character's name in capital letters. Example:

```
                    KAREN
```

Now reset your margins, this time indenting an inch-and-one-half from each side, and type the dialogue, single-spaced under the character's name, this way:

```
                    KAREN
        Dean Taylor, may I speak
        to you a minute?

                 DEAN TAYLOR
        You know the rules, Karen.
        Make an appointment.

                    KAREN
        Please, this is urgent!
        It won't take long.
```

It is important to keep your speeches in this narrow, defined area in order to differentiate the dialogue from the directions, which often extend clear across the page. In teleplay form, parentheses are not used to set off the directions.

When it is necessary to interrupt the dialogue by a direction, it is done in the following manner:

```
                    DEAN TAYLOR
           I'm sorry, but I cannot
           break the rules.  If you'll
           excuse me --

Dean Taylor walks toward the door but
Karen blocks her path.  Karen is
desperate as she pleads with the Dean.

                    KAREN
           You don't understand.
           Please!
```

A good rule to remember is: everything that is *not* dialogue is placed in the *directive* paragraph: camera shots, descriptions of sets, characters, movement—even when there are just a few words. Example:

```
                    DEAN TAYLOR
           Karen, I'm late for an
           appointment.

She glares at Karen.

           If you'll see my secretary,
           she'll tell you when I'm
           free.
```

There is an exception to the non-parentheses rule: When one or two words, at the most, are used as a directive, they can be placed next to the character's name. Lower case letters are used and enclosed in parentheses. Example:

```
        KAREN (quiet anger)
     I have to see you now!
```

Mastering the teleplay form

For an exercise, here's a situation which is the basis for the opening of a television script. See how well you can translate the following prose to teleplay form:

It is a lovely day in early summer. On the patio in a pleasant suburban area, Ginny Holmes, a pretty girl in her early twenties, has rearranged the wicker furniture to accommodate the most important item, a long wooden table which has been transformed into a desk. On it are a typewriter, a ream of paper, and a few pencils in a mug. In a small vase, Ginny places freshly cut flowers.

The screen door of the kitchen leading to the patio swings open, and Bob, an affable man in his late twenties, joins his wife. He is delightfully surprised to see the "desk" and asks Ginny about it. She tells him that it's his new office and ushers him to the chair at the desk. Then she goes on to explain that since he's going to be spending his vacation writing, he should get some sunshine as a bonus. Bob tells her she's a genius. As he kisses her, the phone in the kitchen rings. He goes to answer it.

In the kitchen, Bob talks on the phone to his publisher, George, who inquires about his writing. Bob, looking out of the window as he speaks, tells George he'll have a chapter on his desk soon. The place is conducive to writing. The best part of it is the quiet. There isn't a kid around for miles. He checked before he rented. . . . Bob suddenly stops in the middle of a sentence as he sees a small

boy in the patio talking to his wife. The boy is sticking his grimy
fingers into the typewriter. Bob makes a hurried excuse to George,
hangs up, and quickly walks into the patio to confront the boy.

   Before you start to write these opening scenes in television form,
you may want to refer back to the specific terminology in this
chapter. Remember that scripts are written in the present tense.
Pay close attention to margins, spacing, numbering your scenes
and describing your characters and sets. Don't be discouraged if
you work slowly at first and feel awkward. If you continue to
practice the technique, in a short time it will become second
nature to you.
   As a checkpoint, I am including a sample of the beginning
scenes, but I suggest you refer to it only after you have tried to
work the scenes out by yourself.
   You may want to check your own work against the following
television scenes:

        FADE IN:

1.   EXT. PATIO -- DAY

        It is a lovely morning in early summer.
        The patio is an extension of a modest
        but well-kept house in a pleasant
        suburban area. It faces a small garden
        separated from its neighbors by a white
        picket fence. All the patio furniture--
        chaises, wicker coffee table, chairs--
        looks cool and inviting except for the
        long wooden dining-table which has been
        transformed into a desk. Covered with
        green felt, it holds a typewriter, a
        ream of paper, and a few pencils in a
        mug.

GINNY HOLMES is arranging freshly cut
flowers in a vase which she places on
the desk. GINNY is in her early
twenties, pretty, intelligent. The
screen door of the kitchen swings open
as BOB HOLMES enters frame. BOB is in
his late twenties, affable, nice looking.
He's surprised and delighted to see
Ginny arranging the desk.

                    BOB
         Hey, what have we here!

                    GINNY
         It's your office, darling.
         Try it on for size.

She ushers him into the chair at the desk.

                    BOB
         It's great. But how did
         you -- where did you --

                    GINNY
         Questions, questions! You
         married a genius, that's
         all. I figured if you're
         going to spend your vacation
         writing, you ought to get
         some sunshine as a bonus.

                    BOB
         Ginny, you're fantastic!

                    GINNY (grins)
         I know.

He kisses her. The SOUND of the phone
rings from the kitchen. The ring
continues as Bob finally breaks away.

                    BOB
         I'll get it.

He walks toward the screen door, opens
it.

2.   INT. KITCHEN -- DAY

It is a charming, suburban kitchen with
two large windows that overlook the
patio. The wall-phone is ringing as
Bob walks to it. He answers it and
looks out of the window as he speaks.

                 BOB (in phone)
         Hello ... George, how are
         you? Great. I'll have a
         chapter on your desk
         before --(stops) ... No,
         that's the best part of
         this place. It's quiet.
         Not a kid around for miles.
         I did research before we
         rented it. There's an old
         --(stops)

His face suddenly reflects surprise and
dismay as he looks out of the window.

3.   POV- BOB EXT. PATIO -- DAY

TIMMIE, a five-year-old mischievous-
looking boy, is intrigued with the

typewriter. He places his jam-stained
fingers on the keys.

4.   INT. KITCHEN -- DAY

                    BOB (in phone)
          Listen, George, I'll call
          you right back. Emergency!

5.   EXT. PATIO -- DAY

Bob walks to Timmie as Ginny stands by
with mixed feelings.

III

DRAMATIC CONSTRUCTION

ONE EVENING at a Television Academy "Drop-In" dinner I overheard the following conversation:

> SHE
> Are you a writer?

> HE
> . . . In a way.

> SHE
> What do you write?

> HE (sheepishly)
> The *beginning* of plays.
> I have fourteen unfinished
> manuscripts.

Though his candor was amusing, his situation was not unusual. The fact is, many people have a secret desire to become writers. We all know the man who watches a movie made for television and is convinced his own life story would make a far better drama. In his fantasy he sees himself and his family depicted on the screen by well-known actors. The dream often propels him to the typewriter. Inspired, caught up in the excitement of putting words on paper, he works feverishly as he sets a scene and begins to write the dialogue. "After all," he says to himself, "I know words. I know how people think. All I have to do is listen and write it down." Then why, as in the case of the beginning television playwright, does he stop somewhere along the way, unable to continue?

The answer is obvious. There is more to writing a teleplay than listening to people talk and getting their words on paper. A retentive memory is fine. So is a tape recorder. But dialogue, however authentic, does not of itself make a drama. It is only one of many elements that artfully combined constitute a play.

Basic elements of drama

Beginning playwrights should start by making a list of the basic elements of drama. Though they may be merely words to you now, they will take on meaning as we discuss each one in the course of the book. The important thing is to understand fully that a play is an art form made up of the following essential components:

> theme
> plot
> protagonist
> antagonist
> conflict
> point of attack
> exposition
> crisis
> climax
> mortar
> characterization
> dialogue
> resolution

As we examine each of these terms, we shall, in effect, be cutting through a play, studying the anatomy and learning its basic structure.

From the earliest Greek plays, this structure has endured. Certainly through the years there have been variations in style, concept, costume, and dialogue—but the *basic elements* apply to television plays today, for the dramatic line remains the same. Briefly, the line is a rising one denoting the essential conflict of the characters, building the action scene by scene to its conclusion.

By the end of our analysis, we shall realize that this dramatic line is inherent in all types of drama, comedy as well as tragedy, and it applies to television as much as to the stage.

Naturally, there are exceptions. In our experimental theatre today, traditional structure is changed to allow for different forms of expression. There is the Theatre of the Absurd, of Improvisation, of Audience Participation, and others in which the playwrights are seeking new and different modes of creativity. Like their counterparts, the musicians who write atonal music, these playwrights may be difficult to understand at first, but they have a need to experiment, to do away with conventions and find a new approach. This is all to the good. But they can break form only when they know what it is they are breaking.

It is essential that the aspiring writer know the basics. Once he does, he can then go on to experiment if he wishes. The knowledge of basic dramatic structure, however, will sustain him in his work and give him an excellent foundation.

This is especially true in television writing. Here, more than in any other medium, a rigid discipline is imposed chiefly because of the *clock.* Since sponsors buy segments of time to advertise their products, it is their money mainly that pays for the entertainment shown on the home screen. The television writer, therefore, quickly learns that the time allotted to his play is valuable. He doesn't have the luxury of going off on tangents, aimlessly writing long speeches, and letting the muse, as it were, guide him into some sort of artistic direction. Long before he faces his typewriter, he knows his direction. In the pre-writing period he works out a blueprint of his play much as the architect draws plans before he can begin his construction. (We discuss this thoroughly in subsequent chapters.) To plan a *playable* drama for a specified time slot, the rudiments must be understood.

Talent and discipline

What I have said to this point may sound very restrictive. Words like *limitation, discipline, pre-planning* can be inhibiting to a writer new to this medium, and he will often complain: "I can't work this way. I want to be free to think about art and imagination and creativity. Don't they count at all?"

Of course they do. Without these qualities, the most carefully executed play would be dull and lifeless. It is the talent one brings to his work—the imagination, the enthusiasm—that literally sparks the creative process and fires it into being. But here again, this quality alone without discipline is meaningless. One does not negate the other. Paradoxical as it may seem, talent and discipline are compatible. It is the fusion of both elements that makes the ideal play, for once the planning is finished, the writer is *free* to experience the creative, spontaneous aspects of writing without being shackled by technical details. Only then can he know the joy, the excitement of working on a play whose structure is built on a firm foundation.

For good examples, the aspiring television writer, in addition to watching television plays and films, would be wise to read as many published teleplays as possible. In addition to the collections of current dramas, there are a number of books that came out in the late fifties and early and mid-sixties that included much of the work of the so-called Golden Age television writers. The book, *Television Plays for Writers* (The Writer, Inc.), offers plays by Horton Foote, Rod Serling, Tad Mosel, Reginald Rose, and others. Though the live form in which they wrote is rarely used today, the plays themselves are good examples of the stages of development of television drama.

Motion picture scenarios and stage plays should also be part of your reading list, for television drama is an outgrowth of both these mediums. Here again, the current plays and film scripts can be found in bookshops and libraries—works by Tennessee Williams, Paul Zindel, Edward Albee, Neil Simon, Arthur Miller, and many more. A look at the past will acquaint you with Ibsen whose play, *A Doll's House*, was written in the late 1800s and filmed twice in 1974. It was also a television special that same year, and is likely to be repeated several times in the years to come.

More and more the networks are presenting Specials based on television adaptations of theatrical plays and successful motion pictures. *The Glass Menagerie* by Tennessee Williams was done very effectively not too long ago, starring Katharine Hepburn.

Because stage plays and motion pictures are so closely related to television drama, we will refer to them for illustrations as we explore the principles of dramatic construction.

IV

THE BEGINNING
Blueprint

"TO TAKE the first step. Start . . ." So says Webster in his definition of the word *begin*. It sounds logical, but to a writer, it is often confusing. What in his terms is the *first step?*

In discussing dramatic construction, we listed the elements that constitute a play. Ordinarily, it would be fair to assume that a good starting point would be to investigate each of these terms as they apply to a television play. But this is not the case. Writing a play is an extraordinary situation because we are dealing with creativity and, in the beginning stages at least, it must be given free rein. Imagination, inspiration, enthusiasm, awareness—these are the qualities that cannot and should not be stifled by form at this point. There will be time enough at a later stage to become technical.

But in the beginning, a writer rarely sits down to his typewriter and dispassionately lists the terms of his play in a rational manner.

A teleplay may well result from this process, but because it is written from the *outside in* (rather than from the *inside out*) chances are it will lack the life quality, the spark that illuminates a fine creative work. Let me stress again, in spite of the limits imposed on him, that the television writer must bring this spark to his work, for the medium itself is so keenly alive, so intimate, so immediate that it demands this creative energy and vitality.

27

Granted, a play often falls short on the home screen, but it's this
spontaneous quality that is constantly looked for in the profession
—especially from our new writers.

The question is, how do we capture this elusive thing—this
sudden burst of impressions? Those of you who have had flashes of
inspiration know that the creative mind is anything but orderly. In
the midst of a busy day, snatches of dialogue will dart through
your brain. A character will emerge full-blown and insinuate itself
in your subconscious, waiting to be written. Sometimes a sign in a
shop window will trigger a plot; other times a strong conviction
will stir you, and you are aroused at times by a personal or public
occurrence or event, or images continually playing on your mind
like a kaleidoscope. Let them play. Don't analyze or try to shape
them into something concrete at this stage. These are the images
that are the very life-force of the creative process, and they must
be allowed to burst forth before the reasoning process takes
over.

At what point, then, does a writer *begin* a project? Actually your
creative work starts at the inception of these images. But because
they're elusive, the trick is, at this early stage, to capture them . . .
to put them in safekeeping. There are various methods of doing
this. It is said that Thomas Wolfe, author of *Look Homeward,
Angel,* had a large barrel in his kitchen into which he threw scraps
of paper. Each scrap contained notes about his forthcoming novel,
and it wasn't until the barrel was full that he was ready to begin
the actual writing. Playwright Sylvia Reagen (who wrote *The Fifth
Season*) covers her study walls with pegboard onto which she clips
notes as the idea of her drama evolves. When the pegboard is
crammed, she knows she is ready for the typewriter.

From my own experience, I find a small notebook ideal for the
germination period. For one thing, it's portable, so wherever you
are—in the bus, in the office, in a coffeeshop—you can jot ideas as
they come to you. For another thing, a notebook is self-contained
—an entity—easy to flip through at a moment's notice.

Personal diary

As the impressions accumulate, you are subtly guiding the creative process toward the direction of a completed *blueprint* of your play. An invaluable tool, the blueprint is a personal diary of the *growth* of your play. Jumbled in the beginning, it's a spontaneous outpouring of thoughts, feelings, insights scribbled on the spot just as they come to you, for your eyes alone.

Gradually the scribblings begin to take shape. Questions are answered. Characters are defined. Relationships are established, and even snatches of dialogue are included. Finally, out of these notes, you begin to see the rough sketches of the play, the beginning of structure. The blueprint then becomes a record of the components of the play: the theme, plot, conflict—in fact all the elements previously mentioned as essential. I'm aware that the reader may not know the definition of these terms at this point; but since we are discussing *beginnings*, in the interest of a logical working routine, it is vital to pause at this point to see the significance of the blueprint in the evolution of a play.

As the notebook fills up, the motivations become clear, the characters come alive, and you can see the steady growth, the rising action of the play to its inevitable conclusion.

The following is a sample of the jottings on the first page of a blueprint. Note that the jottings are just that—fleeting impressions of a dinner party I went to, and the germ of a play idea given to me, inadvertently, by my host, Allen:

> Interesting evening—intrigued by what Allen said about new employees of his firm—has been asked by a friend, prison-warden, to consider hiring an ex-con. . . . Allen balks. I always thought he was very liberal but—would *I* hire an ex-con? . . . idea here.
> . . . what if—in the play—there was a judge—distinguished— noted for liberal attitude—writes books on prison reform, makes

speeches . . . what if his best friend—warden—asks him to hire a man soon to be released from prison? . . . beginning of conflict. Judge suddenly realizes even though he is outwardly progressive about reform, when it hits home, he doesn't believe, inwardly . . . what about a son—no, a *daughter.* Good link with ex-prisoner— father tries to keep them apart—girl falls in love—have to work on character of the girl. Who is she? Her feelings about her father? Whose play is it?

V

CATCHING THE VIEWER

THERE'S A considerable difference between the television viewers at home and the people who make a physical effort to get to a play or film. The latter group are much more inclined to be patient at the outset. For one thing, there's the money factor—in some cases a large amount of money if you add up the admission charge to the theatre, parking, dinner and even baby-sitting. This in itself is enough to make people anticipate a good evening's entertainment, and if the play is slow in starting, no one is likely to leave the theatre without giving it a fair chance.

In his own home, however, the television viewer is king. Comfortable in his own surroundings, there is nothing to keep him from turning off your play if it doesn't catch his immediate interest. This is why the beginning of a television drama is especially crucial. Since we are not playing to a captive audience, we have only the opening of our play to intrigue the viewer. If our characters are dull, if the dialogue is static, if the viewer is not involved in the first few minutes, we can be dismissed by the flick of a switch.

How to involve him? By understanding some fundamental concepts about writing.

Conflict

A play never starts at the beginning. It starts "in the middle"—
what Aristotle called *in medias res*—at the point of conflict.

Let's say, for example, that two characters in your play, George
and Diane, have an ideal marriage. They have everything to make
them happy: health, prosperity, a lovely home, two beautiful
children, and their own growing love and devotion to each other.

At this point, they are admirable but hardly subjects for a play.
Why? Because there is no discernible conflict in their lives.
Without it, there is no peg for a drama.

As playwrights, we can construct that peg. Imagine George
announcing to his wife one evening that he's been promoted to
vice-president of his firm. Diane is delighted until she hears the
word *relocation*. Alaska is to be their new home for the next two
years—a fact which excites George and frightens and angers
Diane.

She's tired of being uprooted. After years of moving, she wants
roots for herself and the children. And she wants them now!

George is shocked. He thought he knew his wife. He had always
guessed her reactions correctly before. But now—this seemingly
sudden reversal . . .

It isn't sudden. She tries to make George see this. In the past she
hated moving but she went along with him willingly because it was
necessary. It isn't now. He has enough prestige as chief engineer of
his firm. Why couldn't they go on living peaceably in their present
surroundings? It would be much better for the children—for her.

"And what about me?" George accuses her of not thinking
about his future. He's worked hard for this promotion. He wants
the challenge Alaska offers. What about *his* situation? Isn't she
being selfish?

Isn't he?

An argument follows. Not a trifling argument about her
recklessly buying a new hat or his forgetting to put up the storm

windows. This argument is the beginning of a controversy affecting their marriage, their future. It is a conflict that will continue throughout the play, building in intensity—and it will be—must be—resolved at the end of the play. Should its solution come early, the play would collapse. Conflict is the backbone, the sustaining element of a drama. Without it, there is only a limp series of static events that lead to no logical conclusion.

Not all conflict is as direct as the George and Diane example, in which each character reveals his inner emotions in order to deal with the problem. Some plays present more subtle conflicts—those in which a character has an *inner* struggle. In the award-winning play *That Certain Summer,* written by Levinson and Link, a boy spends his vacation with his father who is divorced. (Hal Holbrook played the father.) Gradually, the boy runs the gamut of emotions from a mild irritation at his father's male friend, to jealousy, apprehension, confusion, and finally horror as he is forced to face the fact that his father is a homosexual. In this case, the conflict which is in the boy triggers the revelation of a secret the father had hoped to keep from him.

Point of attack

The play proper begins the moment the conflict starts—and this moment is called the *point of attack.*

Everything up to this point is merely preliminary to setting the scene for conflict as mood is established and characters are defined. In the theatre, as mentioned before, these preliminaries may go on for several minutes of playing time; but in television drama the point of attack should start as soon as possible, preferably in your typed script on page three. This is easily done if you start your play "in the middle," close to the beginning of conflict. In the George and Diane drama, the first two pages can establish the serenity of the home. It is early evening. The boys come bursting in from baseball. There is good-humored banter between Diane and her two small sons. They remind her to ask Dad (as soon as he comes home) for permission to go on a hiking trip next week. Into this atmosphere George enters and jubilantly announces his promotion. Diane shows interest, but she is not enthused. Promotions in the past meant a change of life style as well as relocation. Naturally she is apprehensive. When George tells her their new home will be in Alaska, she reacts vehemently. The point of attack starts—the conflict is established—and the play has begun in a very short time.

That Certain Summer, the drama about the boy and his father who is divorced, opens with the boy's anticipation of visiting his dad whom he has always adored. The point of attack is at dinner when the mere presence of his father's friend irritates the boy. This is jealousy—nothing more at the time—but it is the beginning of the essential conflict that grows so dramatically, so inevitably to the conclusion of the play.

Many aspiring television playwrights ignore this advice about starting a play as close to the beginning of the conflict as possible; they write pages of dialogue before they reach the point of attack. "Just wait till you get to the end of the scene," they say. "There's a great moment of conflict there."

That conflict may be great when it comes, but, unfortunately, it is too many pages away from the beginning. The equivalent playing time is much too long for a television viewer to wait— especially when there's another channel he can turn to.

Protagonist, antagonist

Since conflict denotes a struggle for victory, it follows that the characters involved in the conflict are on opposing sides. In its simplest form, the prize fight is a good example. Here, two men as equally matched as possible test their strength and skill in a boxing ring while the audience cheers wildly for the fighter of its choice.

With each succeeding round, the excitement mounts, for no one knows who the victor will be.

This is not true in drama. Long before the play is written, there is one person who knows who will "win"—the author. Or, to put it another way, the author knows whose play it is.

The Western movie exemplifies this in its most elementary form. The author pits the "good guy" against the "bad guy" and the audience naturally roots for the good guy. It is he who is the protagonist. From this, one can come to the conclusion that the actor or actress who has the major role in a drama is the protagonist. But such is not always the case.

In a film called *The Prime of Miss Jean Brodie* (based on a novel by Muriel Spark), the leading character played by Maggie Smith is a strange combination of wild romanticism and dogged determination to be an influence on her young girl students. Though her theories are actually dangerous, the girls are caught by her magnetic personality—and one youngster actually loses her life as a result of Miss Brodie's prodding. Throughout the film, we are struck by the unusual character of Jean Brodie—but she is not, in any sense of the word, the protagonist. A young, intelligent student who is not taken in by her sees her as a dangerous element in the school and finally exposes her as a fraud. The student is not nearly so fascinating to watch as Miss Brodie, but it is she (the student) who is the protagonist of the film because we care about her.

The word *care* is the key word here.

The protagonist is the person for whom the audience *cares*.

In television particularly, because the drama is so close to the viewer, the caring quality makes for immediate identification. A case in point—the teleplay *Tell Me Where It Hurts*, by Fay Kanin. In it, Maureen Stapleton plays Connie, a middle-aged wife and mother who feels useless, unloved, and taken for granted by her hard-working, seemingly insensitive husband.

Almost immediately in the Fay Kanin teleplay, the viewer is drawn to Connie, who tries to find answers to her restlessness—

her unhappiness. We care as she learns some facts about modern life from her teen-age daughter; we care as she creates her own consciousness-raising group and talks out her problems with her women friends. We are *with* her as she studies, probes, and gets new insights into herself not only as a wife and mother but as a woman in her own right; and we see her husband's bewilderment as all this happens and the tension in their marriage grows. When she finally lands a job, she meets her husband on a new level. Toward the end of the teleplay, there is a touching scene in which husband and wife save their marriage with a new awareness of each other—and themselves.

Throughout the play, Connie is a true protagonist. She arouses our interest because, among other things, there is nothing passive about her. She is a doer—aware of her problems and anxious to find the solutions—which brings us back to our definition: *The protagonist is the person for whom the audience cares.*

Incidentally, there has been much controversy about the definition of protagonist, antagonist. Perhaps my definition does not concur with others you have read. Frankly, it doesn't matter. The important thing is, does the definition work for you?

The antagonist is the person (or thing) opposing the protagonist.

The antagonist is not always a person. It can be a force: an earthquake, a flood, a blizzard against which the protagonist must fight.

Sometimes, as in the case of an inner struggle, the antagonist and protagonist are imprisoned in the same person. The young boy in *That Certain Summer* is an excellent example. On one level, the boy is the protagonist and his father is the antagonist. But on a deeper level the audience cares about the father, too. Here are people caught in an inexorable situation. The boy is unable to deal with his mixed emotions of love and hate, and is shattered at the end of the play when he finally returns to his mother.

VI

EXPOSITION

Dropping in on Strangers

HAVE YOU ever thought of yourself as an eavesdropper? Inadvertently, we all are, whether we live in a big city or a small town. Ride in a crowded bus, and you cannot help overhearing snatches of conversation. This woman is telling about her operation; that man is complaining about his work. In a restaurant, a couple is discussing a serious family matter. Next to them, a mother is reprimanding her teen-age daughter. . . . And so it goes. Everywhere people are telling about themselves. To the writer, this *telling* is significant. For a brief moment he is catching a glimpse of the inner lives of strangers.

In a sense, this is what happens when you see a play. You are "dropping in" on strangers—but with one vital difference. Though the dialogue may sound natural, the words have been artfully put together to convey specific information. This "conveying of information" is called *exposition*.

As the play unfolds, we get to know the people we see before us: who they are, their relationship to each other, their work, their dreams. In a well-written play, the lives of these people become so real to us that it's a shock when the play ends and we're catapulted back to reality. For a short time we imagine the characters we've just seen living out their lives.

It takes great skill to make an audience respond this way. The writer must be adept at weaving his exposition so naturally into the fabric of the play that the viewer is never aware of the mechanics.

This was not a consideration for the playwright in the gaslight era. The melodramas at the turn of the century were written and acted with bold strokes. On the dimly lighted stage there were no subtleties. Gestures were exaggerated so they could be seen easily. The writing of the play was obvious and usually followed a basic formula. Exposition in those days meant only one thing: *what has happened before the curtain went up.* To give the audience this essential background, it was customary to open the play with a butler and maid. Since the setting was usually a drawing room, it was this room that was polished to a high shine as the hired help revealed vital information to the audience. For example:

> BUTLER: Did you hear what happened to Sir Harry yesterday?
> MAID: Something about a scandal at the bank. Is it true?
> BUTLER: Oh, yes. His uncle, the one who owns a villa in Rome, will be here this week. Sir Harry may be cut off from the family inheritance.
> MAID: But that will be terrible. What about his forthcoming marriage to the beautiful Miss Isabelle?

At the conclusion of the exposition, Sir Harry and Isabelle enter, the servants discreetly exit, and the play proper begins.

As electric lights replaced the gaslight fixtures, the stage took on a new and more vital significance. Exaggerated gestures once so necessary for visibility looked ludicrous now. And the antiquated structure of the play became cumbersome. *Naturalism* became the key word. People were real, not cardboard figures. The traditional drawing room was no longer adequate to house the new plays. In those early days (in the twenties and thirties), playwrights like Elmer Rice and Clifford Odets broke new ground. Rice's *Street Scene* depicted life in the slums of New York. Odets wrote about people struggling against the depression. More and more the new playwrights discarded the old forms, and a new structure—a *totality* of drama—emerged.

How did this change affect *exposition*? The word itself took on a new, expanded meaning. Today exposition starts when the curtain goes up—or, in television and in the movies, when the light on the screen fades in—and it ends when the curtain goes down, or when the light on the TV screen fades out. Everything in the play—the sets, the characters' clothing, their gestures, their dialogue—*every-thing* becomes part of the conveyance of vital information.

Naturally, it is more difficult for the writer to handle this concept. In television, for example, a writer can no longer rely on minor characters or a narrator to explain the background of the play to the viewer. Years ago the old radio daytime serials always began with a honey-toned announcer who brought the listener up to date on yesterday's happenings. Compare this method with our modern daytime television soap operas that start each day's episode *cold*—with no introduction—involving the viewer instantly in the dramatic action and at the same time, through carefully planned dialogue, giving the background of the series as well.

In every type of television play—comedy, drama, a movie made for television—the characters must convey vital information as an integral part of the play's structure, and at the same time, the conflict must be established and the plot line must move forward.

Now let's break down the various aspects of exposition and see how effectively they can be used by the playwright.

Setting

Houses, it has been said, are reflections of the people who live in them. The furniture, the color scheme, the accessories—all the details reveal something about the occupant.

This applies to drama as well. A set can tell a great deal about the play's characters even before they're introduced to the audience. For example, in *Come Back Little Sheba*, William Inge allowed us to take in all the details of the set before we met the major character, played by Shirley Booth. In the movie version, the camera panned to the details of the set: the disordered living room, the film magazines lying about, a box of chocolates, a radio. . . . In the kitchen, we saw a sink full of dirty dishes and a profusion of plants on the windowsill, carefully tended. So far, from the set alone, what do we know about the woman of the house? She is a romantic, a daydreamer, a bad housekeeper, and a lover of nature. She is, in fact, a childlike person with an aura of faded glamour.

In the play (and in the film as well), she makes her entrance from the upstairs bedroom. As she comes down the steps leading into the living room, we see first the slippers with the faded pompons; then the bathrobe or *wrapper* (as it was called in the thirties) with the fake marabou fur framing the florid, middle-aged, kindly face. She moves into the room, snaps on the radio to dance music, pops a chocolate into her mouth, and glances at a movie magazine. It is as if she is reluctant to start the business of cleaning up and getting her day in order. At the kitchen sink she pauses to water her plants. She ignores the dirty dishes. There is no dialogue spoken, but the audience is getting to know this woman whose surroundings reflect her so vividly.

In the early episodes of *The Mary Tyler Moore Show* in which Rhoda was an ugly duckling, there was an interesting contrast between the two girls' apartments. Mary's had a style. It was trim, orderly, feminine—much like its occupant. Rhoda's, on the other hand, seemed to be spilling over with odds and ends. It was casual, bordering on messy, and it reflected her dissatisfaction with herself at that time.

The screen, even more than the stage, affords an excellent chance to use a set for expository purposes. The camera can not only point up important details but establish a mood as well. In a teleplay I wrote—*Double in Ivory*—about a faded concert artist, the camera panned around the studio of the pianist before we actually saw her. We heard the music, Chopin's *Revolutionary Etude*, which was a form of exposition in itself, because it established the anger, the pent-up passion of the woman at the piano. But we didn't see her until we examined the details of the room: the busts of several composers, the pile of sheet music, the pictures and press clippings on the wall, the metronome on the piano, and finally, the strong fingers of the artist at the keyboard. When the camera panned to her face, we saw the strength and frustration that were so much a part of her character.

Gestures

Gestures, the stance, the walk of a character can establish an immediate impression and clue in the audience about the person.

Take Katharine Hepburn's portrayal of Amanda in the television version of Tennessee Williams' play, *The Glass Menagerie*. In the scene in which she greets the Gentleman Caller, Miss Hepburn affects the faded Southern belle. Dressed in chiffon, she "floats" into the room, extending a delicate hand to her guest. With her grace, her gestures, she is (in her own mind) the epitome of Southern refinement and culture. Played against the shabbiness of her actual existence, these affectations heighten the poignancy of the scene.

In contrast, do you remember Anthony Quinn's vivid portrayal of Zorba in the movie, *Zorba the Greek*? From the moment we see him on the screen, we sense his vibrancy. He doesn't walk. He strides. And we can feel the pent-up energy, the animal vitality. His smile is disarming—a combination of tenderness and strength. Everything about him is charged with a love, an exuberance for life.

So much for the non-spoken exposition. Now let's go to the exposition-by-dialogue.

Dialogue

1. *The "strangers-when-we-meet" exposition*
If the characters in the play are strangers, the exposition is easily written because the two people are legitimately asking each other questions the way strangers do in real life. For example:

```
INT. PLANE -- DAY

GEORGE REYNOLDS, an attractive business-
man in his middle thirties, sits
opposite LYNN HARRIS, a pretty woman in
her late twenties.  Lynn is obviously
frightened of flying.  She is clutching
the arms of her seat and is unaware of
GEORGE who pretends to be reading a
magazine, but is actually observing her.
As the plane completes the take-off,
the "FASTEN YOUR SEAT BELTS" sign goes
off.  Lynn takes a deep breath.

          GEORGE
     You did a good job.  Got
     us up fine.

          LYNN
     I...beg your pardon?

          GEORGE
     Body English.  You work
     with the pilot on take-
     offs.

          LYNN (smiles)
     It shows, doesn't it?
```

                    GEORGE
    That you're a bit nervous?

                    LYNN
    I'm terrified!

                    GEORGE
    Is this your first flight?

                    LYNN
    Yes. It's business. I'm
    a buyer for a New York
    department store. (beat)
    Do you fly a lot?

                    GEORGE
    Every few months. Mine's
    business too. I'm a
    consultant for an
    engineering firm.

And on it goes. As these two people ask questions and get to
know each other, the audience gets to know them too. The
exposition is simple because it is natural. An adept playwright
doesn't stop here, however. He must be careful to carry the plot
line forward as the characters reveal facts about themselves.

On the other hand, it is not always necessary to disclose
everything about a character the minute we meet him. In a movie
called *Two People*, a beautiful girl becomes involved with a
sensitive young man. Both are American. Both are traveling from
Marrakech to Paris and then on to New York. The girl tells him
everything about herself: She is a successful model; she is not
married, but she has a child she loves dearly. She is restless, eager
for love but has never really known it. She is intensely attracted to
the young man who is maddening to her because he is so secretive.

The author of the film has purposely held back on the man's

exposition. We know he is in some sort of trouble. He has no passport, but he carries a letter from an embassy official which allows him to travel. Though he is physically attracted to the girl, he rejects her advances and gives her no logical reason for being so withdrawn. The girl is annoyed, curious, even angry at times because she is, in spite of herself, falling in love with him. Before they reach Paris, she finally learns that he is a war deserter, has lived in hiding for three years, and is now going back to the States to give himself up. With the prospect of a prison sentence facing him as soon as he returns, he is naturally reluctant to start a love affair that will lead nowhere. He is fearful of becoming involved.

In this instance, the author has handled exposition like a *spool of thread*, unwinding a little of it at a time. Holding back on disclosures about one character intrigues the other character—and the audience as well. This is permissible as long as there is no confusion. It is good to intrigue an audience, to involve them. But for only a limited time. The author must know when to unwind the spool and let his characters grapple with their circumstances.

2. The "familiar" exposition

When the characters involved are *not* strangers, expository dialogue becomes much more of a challenge. The author must convey information to the audience through the dialogue of people who are *already aware of the information*. For example, a husband and wife are discussing the future visit of the wife's mother. Let's assume that it's important for the audience to know that the mother has certain negative traits: She is bossy, possessive, constantly complaining, and tends to treat her daughter like a child. It is impossible for the couple to discuss these traits naturally without having it sound like forced exposition.

Fortunately there is a simple way of handling this type of exposition. The key word is *emotion*. Once we add emotion to the scene, facts can be revealed easily. The husband's anger allows him to state his objections to the mother's visit. The wife can now react, not to the facts (which she knows) but to the anger generated by her husband. The scene takes on an added dimension because it moves the story forward at the same time that it is revealing information. As an example, let's pick up the scene when the couple discuss the letter from the wife's mother:

                        KEN
          I have a feeling I'm going
          to be out of town those
          two weeks -- on business.

                        JOAN
          How very convenient.

                        KEN
          Well, you must admit it's
          better than staying here
          and having a breakdown.

                        JOAN
          Aren't you exaggerating a
          little?

                        KEN
          Aren't you forgetting a
          lot? Think back, Joan --
          that last visit. Your
          mother wasn't in the house
          ten minutes and there was
          absolute chaos -- she,
          shouting -- you,crying...

                        JOAN
          O.K. I admit she's not
          easy.

                        KEN
          She's impossible! She's
          got the soul of a staff
          sergeant.

                    JOAN
Ken, she's all of five
feet-

                    KEN
Five feet of aggressive,
possessive-

              JOAN (cuts in)
Stop it!

                    KEN
You may as well face it.
Your mother is a self-
indulgent, overbearing-

                    JOAN
I said stop it!

                    KEN
Honey, I don't want to
sound cruel, but think
back on her last visit.
The arguments--the
complaining-

                    JOAN
She doesn't mean it, Ken.
It's just her way.

                    KEN
Remind yourself of that when
she treats you like a little
girl. When she tells you
how to run your home-

              JOAN (cuts in)
O.K. I don't like her
visits any more than you

do. But what can I do
about it? (pause) would
you mind telling me?

KEN
Level with her. Have it
out. Tell her, as nicely
as you can-

JOAN
That "we don't want you
here, dear mother"... is
that nice enough?

KEN
I didn't say it was going
to be easy.

JOAN
Look, Ken, I'm all she has.
If Dad were alive...

KEN
I know. But she's going
to destroy you just the
way she-

He stops as she looks at him sharply.
He deliberately changes the subject.

KEN
Come on...let's have some
coffee.

JOAN
I don't want any.

Joan fights back the tears as she heads
for the bedroom.

```
                    KEN
           Joan...Joanie, listen.
```

He goes after her.

```
                                    FADE OUT
```

3. *Nostalgic exposition*

Nostalgia, when used sparingly, is very effective in building a
full-dimensional character. A woman of thirty in a television play
is much more realistic to viewers if they can catch an occasional
glimpse of what she was like as a child. A few well-chosen lines
spoken in a nostalgic tone set a mood and, at the same time, give
us specific information about the person's background. Here are
several examples of nostalgic exposition taken from a play, *That
One Day*, by Belle Rosow.

Sophie, a vibrant woman in her mid-forties, is standing on
a dilapidated veranda of an old beach house. As she waters her
plants, she talks to her elderly Uncle Jake:

```
                    SOPHIE
           Why don't they grow!
           Dammit, nothing grows
           around here!

                    JAKE
           Who grows flowers in the
           sand?

                    SOPHIE
           My father could.  When I
           was a little girl I used
           to sit on that step, dry-
           ing my hair in the sun,
           while he tended the
           flowers.  They were all
           over the place...so
           beautiful.  Now look at it.
```

Later on in the scene, Jake has his moment of nostalgia. Sophie, still in a dreamy mood, leads him into it.

                    SOPHIE
          They say that in Portugal
          they still have cobblestone
          streets...donkeys and carts
          ... In the spring women
          wear real flowers in their
          hair.

                    JAKE (pause)
          When I was a little boy in
          Yassy, Rumania... would
          come on a certain morning
          every year a little bird
          and sit on my window. By
          this sign, I would know
          it's spring. (pause)
          Sixty-five years ago...
          would you believe it?
          Sixty-five years...

     He takes his glasses off, wipes them,
     replaces them.

          It's getting cold, Sophie.

Much later in the play, David, Sophie's husband, is talking to Uncle Jake. Here we not only sense a nostalgic mood, but we learn very specific information about David's mother.

                    DAVID
          She was in love with romance.
          .. Used to save up pennies
          from the house money --
          spend it on movie magazines...
          I remember long afternoons

```
she spent dreaming over them
by the window. (pause) She
took me with her on secret
trips to the movies -- they
were life to her -- warning
me not to tell my father...
As if I would!
```

One of the most poignant moments in Garson Kanin's play, *Born Yesterday*, which was made into a film with Judy Holliday and Paul Douglas, comes when Billie Dawn talks about her childhood. She remembers her father reminding her to have a hot lunch. In a very short speech, Billie gives us an insight into her *feeling* about her father—her love for him—how she remembers him. Her nostalgia lends her a softness, and as we view her and like her, we become aware of her new-found sensitivity.

But nostalgia is not always sweet. It can be bitter. See how this speech spoken by a forty-year-old woman executive gives us a portrait of the angry child she was:

```
          PAULA
We never had much money
when I was growing up.
But there was always money
for piano lessons. My
mother insisted on that!
Two dollars a week for
the teacher. But if I
wanted a new dress -- do
you know I went all through
high school with one skirt
and two blouses? Clothes
were a luxury. And as for
lipstick and curlers -- they
didn't matter. Only the
brain was important... So
```

```
I grew up awkward and ugly
and no boy ever looked at
me.  And the worst of it
was, I couldn't tell my
mother how I felt.  She'd
never understand...
```

In this nostalgic dialogue, we get a glimpse of the motivation behind the successful executive. There is also the establishment of character relationship and the mother's strong influence in Paula's life.

VII

THEME AND PLOT

TWO PEOPLE take a picture of an identical tree in winter. The first person mirrors the tree exactly. The second does much more than this. By showing us the bare branches against the vast sky, he evokes an emotion. I see it as loneliness. Perhaps it says something else to you, but whatever the emotion, we are quick to feel it. . . . Here, then, is communication, a statement over and above the physical details of the picture. The photographer seems to be saying, "There is a starkness, an isolation in winter." This is his theme.

Theme

All art forms have a theme. In a symphony there's a melodic phrase or a series of notes which recur as the basic theme of the work, in different movements, varying often but recognizable. Here again, it is the statement of the composer.

As a writer, what statement do you want to make? Can you in one short phrase state the theme of your play? What prompted you to write it? What are you setting out to prove? Do you know how it will end? Certainly you should have these answers before you go to the typewriter, especially in a medium geared to the clock.

The resolution has a direct bearing on the theme. Since there can be only *one* theme to a play, the author must make his decision concerning the resolution *early* in the planning stage. As an example, let's look again at Diane and George, whose marriage is at stake because of a job promotion for George which means relocation. The play can end in one of two ways:

1. George can give up the promotion and realize his wife's desperate need for roots. However, his inner anger eventually destroys their marriage.

or

2. Diane can realize that even if she wins and they do not relocate, she can, in a sense, lose George by killing his dream. Therefore, her love for him propels her to relocate.

The author chose the second alternative. The family moves to Alaska. Though Diane never says it in so many words, she comes to the conclusion that "home is where the heart is." If this sounds corny, incidentally, let me assure you that most themes are very prosaic. Writers are often upset by this. They don't understand that originality is important in the *dramatization* of the theme— not in the theme itself. I once gave ten students an assignment to write a play based on an identical theme. There were no duplications. I received ten original plays ranging from tragedy to farce, all exemplifying the one theme. A writer brings to his work his special talent, his uniqueness, his craftsmanship. This is what counts. In the hands of a good writer, commonplace phrases like *love conquers all* or *crime does not pay* can become (and often are) the themes of highly original, extraordinary dramas.

Now back to our play about Diane and George. If the author had chosen the first ending in which George acceded to Diane's wishes, it would have been an acceptable play, but the premise would have to be changed. George gives up his promotion in this version. He stays in the present community, but something in him dies. Inwardly, he begins to resent Diane for killing the dream. The marriage suffers, then finally deteriorates. The theme (or premise) of this play becomes:

The killing of a dream leads to the deterioration of a marriage.

Note the words *leads to*. I am indebted to the late playwright-teacher Lajos Egri (author of *The Art of Dramatic Writing*) who introduced me to these "action words." Used in the context of a theme, they are the key to the conflict, the protagonist, antagonist, and, most important of all, the resolution. Take the theme, jealousy *leads to* its own destruction.

Instantly we know our antagonist: a jealous person. Obviously he or she is jealous of someone—the protagonist (the person we care about). Conflict is created between them which leads to the eventual destruction of the jealous person. With this simple formula, a few of the components of the play take shape easily.

The question is often asked, "Should the audience be aware of the theme?" Not necessarily. In a good play, the viewer is so involved, he is not at all conscious of the technical aspects of the drama. In retrospect, he may realize its impact, but whether or not he recognizes the theme is unimportant. If the viewer is moved, entertained, stimulated, then the writer has accomplished his purpose. Few people are aware, for example, that Ibsen's *A Doll's House* and *Born Yesterday* are based on the same theme. One is a serious, highly emotional drama; the other is a delightful, highly amusing comedy. But the protagonists in each play are very similar. Both Nora in *A Doll's House* and Billie in *Born Yesterday* are, at the beginning of the play, doll-like creatures. Gradually they begin to gain insight into their situations. They become aware of their environment, the men they've chosen, their own self-image. By the end of the play, they grow strong enough, intelligent enough to take a stand against the particular "tyranny" of which they are victims and declare their independence. The theme for each of these plays is:

Self-knowledge leads to independence.

Perhaps you would word the theme differently. Again, no matter. In your own work it is the one statement that counts—a universal phrase applicable to the play you have in mind. When it finally comes to you in the planning stage, you would be wise to jot it down in your blueprint, for it's the beginning of a definite direction of your drama.

One last word on theme: Does it apply to half-hour television sitcoms (situation comedies) as well as to full-length dramatic series? Emphatically so! What we must realize is that a successful series like *All in the Family* and *The Mary Tyler Moore Show* are good examples of compact writing. Each episode is a small play in itself containing all the elements of dramatic construction including *theme*.

For example, let's review an installment from one of the early *Mary Tyler Moore Shows* in which Mary's well-meaning parents decide to live closer to her and re-establish "the old family ties." Mary, used to being on her own, becomes stifled by their overprotectiveness, but because she is afraid to hurt them, she suffers angrily and silently. Finally, at a confrontation, she blurts out her feelings and asserts herself. She must live her own life! The play ends with a new understanding between Mary and her parents. Stated briefly, the theme is: Honesty leads to independence—or, to put it another way, "To thine own self be true."

Now, let's look at an hour-long series, the popular, long-running *Marcus Welby, M.D.* Here again, though there are continuing characters, each weekly segment is a dramatic entity with its own theme. Consider the episode in which Dr. Welby becomes involved in helping a middle-aged male patient who is "cracking up." The man's business is shaky, his marriage is floundering, and he is fearful that his wife and daughter may learn of his extra-marital affair. Hopeful of restoring his confidence, Dr. Welby promises to help the man straighten out his life. Enter the man's daughter, who inadvertently finds out about the extra-marital affair. Though it is over, the girl is bitterly ashamed of her father and is also angry at Dr. Welby for shielding him. Her hate is so strong, it almost destroys her father, until through Dr. Welby she comes to understand about the frailty of human beings and the importance of forgiveness. With love, the family can begin to build a new life based on trust and understanding. Basically, the theme is: *Love conquers all.* Prosaic? Of course. But let me reiterate: Themes are not of themselves original. The important thing is the *play* that illustrates the theme.

Plot

The plot is the plan of action of a play. We are concerned here with the events of the play, the particular situations that move the story forward—in other words, the *progression* of the scenes. Naturally, in an action play, or what we sometimes refer to in television as a "get-that-car" drama, the movement of the scenes is obvious. Things happen quickly, dramatically—a kidnapping, a chase, a desperate fight on a precipice. This is movement we can see and follow.

A rerun of the well-known Perry Mason series featured a teleplay by Richard Grey, from a story by Erle Stanley Gardner— *The Case of the Green-Eyed Sister.* The plot had all the usual twists and turns of an absorbing mystery teleplay: Plain Harriet Baine has a glamorous sister who, unknown to Harriet, is in cahoots with Harriet's fiancé, the fortune hunter, Addison Doyle. Harriet is worried about her ailing father, whose former partner, J. J. Stanley, is being blackmailed. Apparently these two men embezzled money years ago, and the bank is on to them. Baine visits Stanley with money to pay off the blackmailer. Stanley is killed. Perry Mason is called in on the case and in his inimitable manner traces and finally points to the guilty party—Addison Doyle.

In its genre, the plot moves swiftly, the characters are quickly delineated, suspicion is thrown on each of them, as we study their motivations for murder, and the viewer is intrigued. This is movement in which we can follow the rising action to its exciting conclusion.

But strongly emotional plays have rising action, too—inward action, much more subtle, and charged with a different type of dramatic excitement. Although Ibsen uses blackmail in *A Doll's House*, the blackmail is a device to motivate his heroine, Nora, to face herself honestly. We actually see Nora grow from a childlike person to a woman of depth. These are dramatic events that contribute to her growth, and they might never have happened if the threat of blackmail had not entered the picture. Briefly, let's review the plot: Nora is threatened by a blackmailer, Krogstad, who has just been fired from his job at the bank by Nora's husband, Torvald.

If Nora doesn't help him regain his position, the blackmailer threatens to tell Torvald about a check Nora forged years ago. She needed the money desperately to save her husband's health at that time, and she never told him of the forgery. . . . Nora's pleas to Torvald to restore Krogstad's job go unheeded. He considers his wife a doll-like creature, and he will brook no interference in his business world. The forgery is exposed. Instead of understanding the circumstances, Torvald is furious, conscious only of how this will affect his reputation. Nora gradually sees how shallow, egotistical, and unsympathetic her husband is. She eventually leaves him.

Again, the blackmail triggers the action and is a vital part of the plot. But what happens to Nora *emotionally* and *intellectually* is also part of the plot. We see her react to her husband, to the blackmailer, to her environment. Each time she gets a new insight, she grows as a person—and this growth moves the play forward on a deeper level.

Summing up, the plot answers the question, "What happens?" If you can state the events of the play, the rising action, the character growth, and do it succinctly and interestingly, then you've mastered one of the first requisites of writing for television.

VIII

CRISIS, CLIMAX, AND RESOLUTION

CRISIS

Years ago in the shop windows of almost every drugstore in the country, there was a print of a very popular painting. It depicted a doctor sitting at the bedside of a feverish little girl while her parents looked on anxiously. The painting was called "The Crisis." What it meant in those days before wonder drugs is that at a given time the fever would break and the patient would recover—or the temperature would rise even higher and the child would die. In other words, the crisis was the *turning-point* of the illness.

In the context of drama, the definition is much the same: *The crisis is the turning-point of the play* . . . whether it is a stage play, a theatrical motion picture, or a television play.

We have established that a play starts at the beginning of a conflict and rises in action as the conflict grows. This rising action is the culmination of a series of little crises leading up to the major one—the turning-point. It is then that the "fever" will break and the protagonist will do something about his or her problem. Usually the crisis involves an explosive type of dramatic action, for the character is at fever pitch at this point in the drama. Up to this point, he has tried to be rational, but as the tension mounts, as the situation becomes unbearable, the "explosion" occurs. It is not premeditated. It just happens.

59

Let's look at some examples of crisis from television plays in which this burst of emotion takes over: In the first episode of *Rhoda*, Valerie Harper portrays a love-starved career girl who, in the course of a New York vacation, meets and falls for a personable divorced man, Joe. Rhoda can't bear to go back to Minneapolis at the end of her vacation—so, on an impulse, she phones her employer, pretends to be ill, and then rushes to Joe's office to tell him she has another week in New York. But Joe has a business trip scheduled. Rhoda is shocked, but in all fairness, Joe tries to make her see that he didn't know about her "impulsive gesture." He tries to explain this to Rhoda . . . and then . . . the explosion! Rhoda's disappointment, her anger, her insecurity, and sudden feeling of foolishness result in a tirade! She accuses him of not caring. She lied to her boss because she wanted more time with Joe—but he can't change his business plans. He doesn't care! Well, she doesn't either. She doesn't need this! . . . and on . . . and on. Joe can't stop her. Rhoda can't stop herself. The tirade reaches "fever pitch." Then she storms out of the room. The crisis is over.

On a deeper level, here is another example of crisis, this time from *The Lie*, written especially for television by Ingmar Bergman. In it a husband and wife promise each other to admit infidelity if either of them should be guilty of it. During the course of the drama, the husband has a particularly harrowing day. He goes through a series of crises which affect his job, his health, and his self-image. Toward the end of the day he becomes sexually involved with a young nurse. It is a casual encounter which means absolutely nothing to him; but remembering the pact he made with his wife (whom he loves very much) he feels compelled to admit his transgression. Difficult as it is, he guiltily faces his wife. His confession is a culmination of all the frustration he's been experiencing: his fear of his health waning, of facing middle age, of not being successful at his job. He thinks that by being truthful, by clearing the air, he'll not only be exonerated but the marriage will, in some way, be strengthened. He is in for a shock! His honesty evokes his wife's confession. Disillusioned with marriage, she's been having an affair for years and has kept it secret. . . . Recriminations follow—searing words—and even physical violence, as the couple grope with the painful fact that their marriage is built on a lie.

There is a crucial scene in Robert Anderson's moving play, *Tea and Sympathy*, in which the wife accuses her husband (who is a teacher in a boys' school) of bullying a sensitive student. It is a tense moment led up to by a series of minor crises in which the wife becomes increasingly suspicious of the motive for his harassment of the boy. The husband repeats his hatred of homosexuals; he is certain the boy is one. The wife, unable to restrain her anger, blurts out the truth as she sees it: It is *he*, the husband, who is a latent homosexual, and this is why he detests the boy for reminding him of the very quality he loathes in himself! . . . It is a powerfully explosive scene, just before the second act curtain, and it foreshadows the end of their relationship.

The same subject matter, homosexuality, is treated very effectively in an episode of *All in the Family*. Here are the events leading up to the crisis: Archie makes snide remarks to the family about "sissies." Mike tells him not to judge people superficially, but Archie is not about to give up a prejudice. Later, in the neighborhood bar, Archie meets a handsome, rugged-looking athlete, and is so impressed by the young man, he tells the family about him. Mike knows of—and respects—the athlete, but he cannot help telling Archie that his hero is known to be a homosexual. Mike states it as a fact, and in no way means to degrade him; but Archie becomes furious. He bellows his rage at his "meathead" son-in-law, accuses him of being jealous, and defends his newly-found friendship. The rage reaches "fever pitch," and Archie's explosion strains the already widened breach between them.

In each example, note that the characters, through their emotional outburst, reach a "point of no return" in the play. Something is done, something is said that seems irrevocable. They must then go on from the crisis to the next point in the play, *climax.*

CLIMAX

In the aftermath of emotional outburst, *reason* takes over. Let's continue with the above-mentioned episode from *All in the Family*: Toward the end of the episode, Archie is stunned when the athlete tells him he is a homosexual. There are no histrionics in this scene. Unlike the highly charged crisis, this scene is quiet, almost underplayed. The young man explains himself to Archie and then casually finishes his drink. Archie, shocked, sits at the bar unable to believe what he has been told.

Compared to the emotional outburst of the crisis, the climax seems much lower in tone. It is, nevertheless, *the highest point of the play* in terms of what is happening to the characters. Archie is visibly shaken. His values are no longer eternal verities. And the worst part of it all is that Mike was right, a fact Archie hates to acknowledge.

One of the best examples of climax is seen in the last act of *A Doll's House*. In the spirit of the Christmas season, Nora's husband finally forgives her for having forged a check years ago. The entire incident is put to rest, and the audience assumes this is the end of the play. But Ibsen has planned a startling climax. . . .

Nora does not thank Torvald for his forgiveness. Instead, in a soft voice, almost a whisper, she tells him that she doesn't forgive *him.* At first he cannot believe she is serious. But she goes on. Now that she knows what he is really like, she can no longer live with him. Certainly she cannot accept the old order of being a "doll-wife" to him. Inwardly she has grown as a person, as a woman. She can no longer live with a man who considers her childlike, and who is, himself, shallow and egotistical. Though it means leaving her children, Nora cannot compromise.

This scene, even today, is still one of the most powerful moments in dramatic literature. It is, in every respect, the highest point in the play *in terms of what is happening to the characters.*

Their entire lives are changing. New decisions are being made. Though there will be other problems to face in the future, in the context of the play, this particular conflict is ended. The play is practically over.

RESOLUTION

Resolution is almost self-explanatory. It is, in a sense, the *solving* of the problem, for it comes on the heels of the climax. We can trace the logical steps to it quite simply:

1. We know that a play ends when the conflict ends.
2. In the climax, the protagonist takes action to resolve the problem.
3. Once this action is taken, the conflict ends. The play is almost over.
4. Resolution, therefore, follows on the heels of the climax.

To continue with *A Doll's House*, once Nora announces she is leaving, the play is over. Torvald reacts, of course, but he is so stunned, he can barely talk. Ibsen wisely ended the play at exactly the right moment. Nora leaves to start a new life. From her standpoint, the play ends on a positive note. She is stronger, she has found herself, and though life will be difficult for her, she is ready to accept the challenge. She prefers it to living a lie with her husband.

But resolutions are not necessarily positive. In the teleplay, *The Morning After*, by Richard Matheson, Dick Van Dyke portrays a successful public relations executive with a charming wife, two children, and a comfortable home in the suburbs. Because of his drinking problem, he begins to lose ground: First, the job is threatened. Then his wife leaves him. Though he makes several half-hearted attempts to break the habit, he finally succumbs to it. The last shot of him is on the beach, huddled against the wind, drinking himself into oblivion.

The film, *The Way We Were*, has a poignant resolution. A once-married couple meet on a busy New York street and tell each other about their "new lives." *She* has remarried and says she is very happy. *He* is dating and professes to be happy, too. But the camera lets us know (through the close-ups) that in spite of their words, the old chemistry between them is still very much alive. We know, as they do, however, that life together for them is impossible. So they stand for a moment, smiling, making small talk, and trying to stifle the impulse of telling each other how they really feel.

The movie wisely ends on this scene. Their relationship is over. The film is over. What happens to them in the future may be interesting, but it is of no consequence to *this* film.

When a writer goes on and on, not knowing when his play is over, he creates an *anticlimax*, thus delaying the end and often dissipating the dramatic impact of his play. A good writer knows where to stop.

IX

THE TIE THAT BINDS

ARMED WITH the knowledge of the craft, a beginning television playwright still can become very discouraged. He has every right to expect the technique to work for him, and yet, every once in a while he'll find himself hopelessly blocked at the typewriter.

"I don't get it," he'll say. "I've worked everything out—plot, theme, conflict—but somehow I can't get past the first few scenes. Something's wrong!"

What is usually wrong is the absence of one vital element in the planning stage. I call it *mortar.* The name doesn't matter. What it represents, however, can mean the difference between an adequate play and an exceptional one.

The mortar is that quality that binds the protagonist to the antagonist, making it extremely difficult for the protagonist to get out of a bad situation. If early in the play the characters can face each other and just by talking resolve their problem, there is no play. The author has fooled himself into thinking his conflict was strong enough to sustain a drama. As a result, he invents situations which stretch the action unduly until the climax, when the characters finally come to grips with the problem. It is so easily solved, however, that the viewer feels cheated.

In an architectural context, a building that is constructed

flimsily can be destroyed by the impact of a heavy storm. But a structure carefully designed to withstand pressure will remain intact. Similarly, a play must be built to resist pressure, but in dramatic terms the play must stand up not only in spite of adversity, but *because* of it. This adversity—this conflict—is the mortar that binds.

Emotional forces

A television movie, *Sunshine*, by Carol Sobieski, based on a story by Norma Klein, tells of a young woman's battle against cancer. There is no easy solution here, especially since the play is based on a true story. The viewer knows that the protagonist, Kate Hayden, is going to die. Angry, frustrated, but determined to fight, Kate rails against the disease.

In the broadest sense, the cancer is the mortar of the drama, the element that makes it virtually impossible for the protagonist to resolve the conflict.

But there is another factor—a positive one—that is a cohesive force in the play. It is not Kate's fight against death, but the way she *lives* that last year, that makes the teleplay memorable. A device, a tape recorder, a "diary" of her remaining months, is suggested by Kate's therapist, a compassionate woman, Dr. Gillman. Each day Kate records her thoughts honestly and directly. It keeps her going, living her numbered days intensely, giving meaning to her life. At the end of the play, she has left her mark for her husband and child—her thoughts, her dreams for their future, her love for them. This device, then, is a kind of mortar of its own, a "life-force" binding the protagonist to live to the fullest every day, even though she knows it is impossible to escape her predictable death. The play stands up "not only in spite of adversity, but *because* of it."

In the comedy I mentioned earlier, *Born Yesterday*, Garson Kanin uses mortar in a different way. Let's review the events of

Born Yesterday: Billie, a former chorus girl, lives with a tyrannical, wealthy junk dealer, Harry, who has picked her up "from the gutter" and never lets her forget it. In the course of the play, Harry hires a tutor for Billie to improve her speech. The project backfires. Billie has hidden resources. With her tutor's guidance, she discovers her innate intelligence, a reasoning, questioning mind, and a capacity to love deeply.

Understandably, she wants to leave Harry and start a new life. But we know that if he lets her go, the play is over.

What, then, is the obstacle—the mortar—that makes it difficult for her to escape? Is it love that binds Harry to her? Not really. He is incapable of love. Is it his ego? Perhaps. But ego alone would not make him so adamant about keeping Billie with him. After all, he could always pick up another "broad." What then? . . . The playwright hit upon the one logical factor: his business transactions.

Early in the play Harry orders Billie to sign some papers, which she does, obediently, unquestioningly. Later we learn that Harry's illegal holdings are all in Billie's name. He desperately needs her—and he is not about to release her to live her own life. As long as he has this hold on her, the conflict continues to grow. The mortar is set.

Hate can also be a binding force in a drama. Reginald Rose exemplified this superbly in an early television play, *Tragedy in a Temporary Town*. His setting, a trailer camp in which migrant aircraft workers and their families live. An incident occurs: a mischievous boy forces a kiss on Dotty, the fifteen-year-old daughter of Doran, one of the workers. The girl, shocked and frightened, says she was "grabbed," and the news of the "attack" quickly spreads around the camp.

Doran, a hostile, bitter man, is out to get the boy and he whips up his own hatred by stirring the men into an angry mob. Once the hunt for the boy is on, there is no stopping them. Dotty doesn't remember his face, only the voice when he said, "Hey." Every boy in the camp is questioned. Doran eventually settles on young

Raphael who is innocent, but by this time the mob's fury must be fed. The fact that Raphael is Puerto Rican feeds their prejudice. The men are like animals now, beating the defenseless boy.

At the end of the play, Beggs, the father of the guilty boy, Buddy, turns on the mob and makes them see what "pigs" they are. Shame, humiliation replace hate as the men walk back to their trailers.

In this powerful teleplay, hate is the binding—and the *blinding* —force, the mortar that withstands the pressure until the very end of the drama.

Conversely, a deep love can be the cohesive element in a play. The movie, *A Touch of Class*, began with a frivolous affair between a married man and a divorced woman. The situation became complicated only after they fell in love. In spite of the hazards, the difficulties in seeing each other, they prolonged the affair simply because they could not bear to give each other up. When they finally said goodbye, the movie was over. Their intense love (the mortar that sustained them) had to be dissolved.

Sustaining the vital element

In the writing of your own television play, you can save yourself much time and frustration if, in the planning stage, you give some thought to this vital element. Study your protagonist and antagonist. Then ask yourself what makes it difficult for the protagonist to get out of the conflict. Can it all be resolved by a talk between them?

One of my students had to ask himself these questions after struggling with the opening of his teleplay. On the surface, his plot line had all the features of a good conflict:

A young man, Jerry, brought up in the tradition of the Jewish theatre by his aging uncle, now wants to break into Broadway. His girl friend is the daughter of a famous producer, and she urges him to leave his uncle and start a new career. This is not easy. Jerry owes much to the old man. After the death of his parents, his aunt and uncle adopted him, raised him, and taught him a profession. The girl reminds him that the Jewish theatre is dying. He has to break away!

As painful as it is to him, Jerry tells his uncle about his decision. The uncle is shocked, angry, and very hurt. Jerry leaves.

At this point the author of the play ran into trouble. Up to the confrontation, the scenes worked very well, but he fooled himself into thinking there was a conflict strong enough to sustain the drama. Once Jerry leaves his uncle and aunt to pursue his own career, the play is finished. Moreover, the audience is sympathetic to Jerry. No one can truly fault him for his decision. He's young, talented, ambitious and has a right to follow his star. It's true the uncle is hurt, but eventually he'll get over his anger. The conflict, therefore, is over. The author is blocked.

But he doesn't have to be. The addition of one element—the mortar—can sustain the conflict and strengthen the play.

What if, for example, Jerry is actually part of an act with his uncle? What if they're performing nightly in the last remaining Jewish theatre, and the audience really comes to see Jerry who sings and dances and is, in effect, *the* show?

Now see what happens when Jerry is persuaded by his girl friend to try for Broadway. Leaving his uncle means *depriving him of a living*. The act is dead without Jerry. No one will pay to see the uncle. Aside from the financial loss, there is another thing to consider—the old man's ego, the feeling of himself as a performer. He has nothing else. . . .

Now Jerry's conflict is real. Can he leave his uncle this way? What about the girl friend? She insists that Jerry is sacrificing his career, but she doesn't know what the uncle means to him. Is she the wrong girl for Jerry? Will he be persuaded? And what about the aging uncle? Is it possible that he refuses to see that the Jewish theatre is dead? Is he holding onto tradition, living in the past? Does his wife see this? Does she eventually help to release Jerry?

All these questions bubble up to revitalize the play, to give it more substance, more playable scenes. And this can happen only with the added ingredient that makes it difficult for the protagonist to resolve his conflict. Mortar.

Remember, the stronger the ties that bind, the more powerful the play.

X

CHARACTERIZATION

CAN YOU remember the last time you were bored? It may have been in pleasant surroundings with perfectly nice people, but you were conscious only of the clock barely moving . . . the dull, dead pauses, and your own frozen smile. Afterwards, you may have written off the visit as a wasted evening. No matter. There are other evenings and other people.

As a layman, you can afford to forget a boring evening. But as an aspiring television playwright exploring the components of drama, you can learn a great deal from such an evening. Why was it boring? What was there about these "perfectly nice people" that made you yawn? Did they talk too little—or too much—about personal subjects in which you had no interest? Were they constantly interrupting each other with unimportant details:

"No, dear, that's not when it happened. It was *Tuesday*, not Monday. I remember because I was on my way to the dentist. . . ."

Did they go on interminably showing slides of their last trip to Mexico? (You had been there, and you had your own slides.) In short, what did all this add up to in terms of your general reaction? Would it be safe to say you *didn't care?*

In drama, we *must* care. It is the key to characterization—caring about the people in your play and making the viewers care.

Think of it this way: You, the writer, are asking an audience to spend an evening with people you've created. If the people are uninteresting, if their dialogue is static, if their problems are inconsequential, the viewers will be bored—and this leads to irritation, not involvement. Fortunately for them, they can escape simply by turning the dial.

The playwright, therefore, must create three-dimensional people whose traits are individualized, who grapple with problems in a dramatic way. Selectivity becomes the primary tool of the writer in creating these characters, who must be true to themselves, living out the pattern of their own personalities in the course of the teleplay's development.

The question is, how does the writer find these characters? By taking them from real life? To beginning writers this may seem obvious and logical. Write about someone you know and place him in a real situation. Simple. How can you go wrong? Easily! Actually, this is how trouble begins. Real people have a way of taking over a script. *They,* not *you,* become the masters of the situation. They refuse to conform to a dramatic line in the planning stage. Often a student allows his play to dwindle off into a meaningless ending because his protagonist never takes the necessary action to fulfill his theme. In his defense, the writer will insist:

"I *know* this person. She wouldn't take a stand on anything."

The appearance of reality

Perhaps in reality the character would be wishy-washy. But the salient point here is that once she becomes a character in an original play, she is *not* a real person. She must only be created to appear to be so. This gives the writer a freedom he can never have if he is burdened by the image of the actual person who refuses to be molded to the play's dramatic needs. The writer must have flexibility and he can achieve this only if he creates his own characters.

This does not mean, however, that you cannot borrow certain traits from real people. A voice, a gesture, an attitude can enhance the character you have in mind. This is why it is so essential to observe keenly the human condition, at the same time remembering that it is *you* creating the person in your mind. Again, I like to think of the analogy of working with clay, shaping, molding, restructuring if necessary, until the image is right and the characters in the television script look as if they have lives of their own.

Certainly in drama, a well-rounded or three-dimensional character must have a semblance of real life. This is achieved first by recognizing that he or she did not spring full-blown into your play; and second, by inventing a family history—a background for your character. If, for example, your protagonist is a woman of thirty-three, you have to keep in mind that she was once sixteen—and ten—and an infant. As a writer, you must know the factors that contributed to her development as a person in your play. In short, you must know this creation of yours in every aspect, because it is only then that she can fulfill her function in your script.

Biographies of characters

This is why I urge beginners to write biographies of their characters—the two major ones at least—protagonist and antagonist. These biographies should be included in your blueprint of your television play as a basic part of the planning stage. They should cover all the details: infancy, childhood, schooling, adolescence, personality traits, feelings, parents—everything you can think of that will add up to the total person in your play.

Since you write these biographies for yourself alone, they can be

written in any style you like. Perhaps you prefer a monologue of
the character speaking. For example:

> I don't believe that people change a great deal. I'm thirty-three and
> I have to admit I still have the same longings I had as a child . . . to
> feel secure—special—to be admired for something. I never was. . . .
> All the time I was growing up . . . I used to hear people say, "She's
> so plain"—and they'd look at my mother with surprise. *She* was the
> beauty—my mother. And she had a kind of a . . . glow about her, a
> vivacity that made her exciting. Next to her, I was nothing. And she
> knew it. Even when I was a toddler, I think I could sense her
> disappointment. *Plain.* How I hated that word!

The monologue could go on for as many pages as it takes to get a
comprehensive history of this character.

If you prefer straight narrative, this is equally acceptable. For
example:

> Judith Heller doesn't believe people change a great deal. At
> thirty-three, she has to admit that she still has all the longings she
> had as a child—to feel secure—special, etc.

Once more, let me assure you that the style of the biography
doesn't matter. Its content does. As part of the blueprint, it's for
your eyes alone to help you define the people in your play.

Incidentally, if you find it difficult to invent a background, the
simple word *why* may help you enormously. As an exercise, try
making a statement about your character. Then ask yourself
"why." The question will lead into another statement which will
lead into another "why," and so on. For example:

> Thirty-three-year-old Judith Heller is shy, very reserved in the
> presence of others.

Why?

> As a child she was very plain. Her mother was beautiful, vivacious.
> Judy seemed to fade into the background.

Why?

Judy has never had a chance to express herself. Her mother was too dominant a personality. Judy could never live up to her.

Why?

Even as a toddler, she knew she was plain. She developed a bad self-image, one she never lost as an adult.

Why?

New insights

This method uncovers layer after layer of the personality of the child who grew up and who, you might say, found her way into your script.

Often the biography gives you keen insights, not only into that particular character, but others as well. In this instance, the mother is already emerging as a dominant personality. Perhaps she appears in your play as a woman of sixty. She is obviously still dynamic and may have traces of the beauty she once had. Does she still make her daughter uncomfortable? Is there the old tension between them? By the time you have completed the daughter's biography, you will know her present feelings about her mother. The scenes in which they appear together will be forceful because you, the playwright, have created a depth of character for them, and yet, in a strange way, it has become entirely their own. From the seed of an idea, therefore, you can breathe life into a character that appears to work out its own destiny.

Study the people in the splendid British television import, *Upstairs, Downstairs,* and see how quickly, how perfectly the characters are drawn. The "downstairs" staff of servants are not merely butlers, footmen, and maids. Each is a *person,* uniquely himself or herself with definite characteristics. Rose, the maid, is serious, guileless, and prim. Similarly, the cook, the butler, the scullery maid are all drawn with careful attention to detail. Their speech, their gestures, their outlook on life give us an instant awareness of their individual characters.

The same holds true for the "upstairs" people. Each member of the distinguished family emerges as a real person with distinctive human foibles. The son has his moments of weakness, the daughter, her rebelliousness; father tries to live up to being the Lord of the Manor, but sometimes falters, and his beautiful, gracious wife sometimes is stubborn and quick-tempered. These are the people who week after week on the television screen impress you with their *reality*. They are, in every way, fully realized by their television creators, and they do, indeed, give a sense of *working out their own destinies*.

As a matter of fact, this is true for many continuing characters in other established television series: Marcus Welby, Maude, Mary Richards (played by Mary Tyler Moore), Archie Bunker, to name a few, were all meticulously devised before the actual series began. It was imperative for the creators of the shows to know every detail—everything pertinent to the main character. Once on the air, each segment is drawn to reinforce the character and add to the individual plot line. As the weeks go by, the character becomes so fully realized that the viewer anticipates certain reactions to specific situations. Archie Bunker, for example, is bound to be prejudiced. Mary Tyler Moore sooner or later overextends herself, and Rhoda is always vulnerable.

In original television dramas (a "special" or a "movie made for television"), the writer can use more playing time to develop his characters. But these characters must be fully developed, three-dimensional people, because there is no chance for reinforcement the following week. They have only sixty or ninety minutes in which to make an impression. And that impression can be vivid only if the writer has done his preliminary work carefully. Through the biographies, he can know them, and this knowledge will help him to create interesting people, easily identifiable and consistently true to themselves. In teleplays like *Brian's Song, I Heard the Owl Call My Name,* and *Teacher, Teacher,* the characters are memorable. In the latter, for example, we meet a retarded child who is enormously affected by a dedicated young teacher. Here are a man and a boy with a world of difference between them—but the man reaches out to the child, convinced he is "teachable." And the boy, in spite of his handicap, begins to respond. It is several years since this play, written by Allan Sloane, was presented on television, but this boy and his teacher are not easily erased from the mind.

Still, beginners are often tempted to write about characters on a much grander scale: power-hungry tycoons, notorious gangsters, international spies, because to the novice these characters offer rich opportunities for tense drama. In some cases, this is undoubtedly true, but it is equally true that the common man has the makings of absorbing drama, especially for television, because this medium allows us such an *intimate* look at ourselves.

Consider Paddy Chayefsky's Bronx butcher who made television history in the play called *Marty.* He was shy, awkward, unattractive, but there was something about him—a desire to break the mold, to fight the loneliness, to reach out to life—that made him *worth writing about.* Chayefsky let us identify with his loneliness. We cared about his struggle to overcome it, and we were gladdened by his emergence as a person who had the courage to love. In short, Marty was worth the caring.

Will we care? This is the question you must ask about the characters *you* are creating. The time you take getting to know them will be well spent, especially before you get to the typewriter.

XI

DIALOGUE

ONE OF the first assignments I give my students is to listen to people talk and faithfully write what they hear. In the supermarket, the bus, a crowded elevator, an office—wherever they happen to be, I ask them to "eavesdrop" and record the words to the best of their memory. No editing. No reshaping. They are to bring in "natural" dialogue.

Sometimes they're rewarded with a delightful turn of phrase, an original thought; but for the most part, they are forced to the conclusion that verbatim natural dialogue is dull. They discover that vocabulary is limited, unoriginal, repetitious, and that people generally are much more anxious to talk than to listen.

If we were to tape-record our own dialogue for a week, we would probably be shocked at our limited number of words: *How are you? Let's have lunch. Have a nice weekend. Did you have a nice weekend?*

An original phrase is the exception, not the rule. This is because the pressure of daily living stifles our creativity. Most of us are caught up in the mundane routine of going to work and coming home again, and we use the minimum amount of words to get us through the day. So, to repeat, we conclude that natural dialogue is dull.

And yet, aren't we striving for naturalism when we write a play?

Not exactly. Our aim is the *semblance* of naturalism. We want the characters to *sound* real, but the very nature of drama—the compression of time and space—demands a certain artfulness. It's much like a woman's clever use of cosmetics to achieve what is known as the "natural look." Her admirers little realize how much careful preparation goes into the no-make-up face.

Preparation is the key to design in any medium. In writing dialogue, the playwright can do his preliminary work in the market place. It is helpful to look, to listen, to observe the human condition at all times, as long as one remembers that it is in the *second* step—the refining process—that the artistry comes through.

There is nothing haphazard about good dramatic dialogue. When it sounds right, it is the result of a combination of factors. One of them is the writer's keen ear and perception of people.

The more you know the character in your play, the easier it is for the character to help *write his own dialogue.* Though this sounds mystical, I assure you it is precisely what happens. This is why I have urged you to write a biography to acquaint yourself thoroughly with the character's background. Once you have done this, see him in your mind's eye as he appears in your drama. Know what he looks like, how he moves, what he thinks. Imagine the sound of the character's voice, the timber, the inflection. Now put him into a dramatic situation and *let him talk. Aloud. Through you.* The results will astound you.

Take, for example, a character in a teleplay called *My Father Talks to Statues* (a collaboration between Phyllis Coe and myself). Phyllis Coe created a delightful character, Janos Miklos, on whom the play was based. Here is the original description of him:

"Janos is a Saroyan-like character—a sculptor. A free spirit, he bows to no man and runs according to his own time clock. Larger than life in every way, he's a big, bearded man burning with energy and opinions. His voice is booming, his clothes are wrinkled, his humor is rich and aphoristic."

Even before you read a sample of his dialogue, can you hear Janos talk? The author obviously could.

As you read the dialogue between Janos and his son, Joey, see how Janos' speeches exemplify the author's description:

```
INT. STUDIO BASEMENT -- NIGHT

The room is equipped on one side with
futuristic statues.  On the other, it
is furnished with bare essentials for
living:  a kitchen table, three chairs,
a gas ring for cooking, a small
portable refrigerator (broken down).

JOEY, a wistful nine-year-old, is
preparing dinner.  He stirs a non-
descript stew in a pan on the gas ring.
It is on the verge of burning.

Janos enters.

                    JANOS
          What is that smelling like
          a boiled boot?

Janos sweeps across the room, drops his
packages on the kitchen table.

                    JOEY
          I burned the dinner, Poppa.

                    JANOS
          Don't look so sad.  There'll
          be other dinners.

He takes a close look at Joey.
```

                    JANOS
          Hey, Longface, I said it
          didn't matter. Don't you
          feel well?

                    JOEY
          I'm all right.

Joey tries to busy himself, avoiding
Janos' look. Janos sits down on a
kitchen chair, pulls Joey close.

                    JANOS
          Come here, my poor man's
          treasure.

                    JOEY
          I'm not a treasure.

                    JANOS
          Sure you are. Youth is
          treasure. Truth is treasure.
          You are youthful. You are
          the most truthful boy I know,
          and as you grow, you shine...
          Now, look what I brought
          home.

He begins to unwrap packages.

          You know this is payday at
          the art school where I am
          instructed to destroy any
          signs of talent in the
          young.

```
            JOEY
You didn't spend all the
money, Poppa?


            JANOS
I didn't spend any.  On
the way home, the butcher
called me in to fix the
lettering on his sign and
he gave me this!
```

Triumphant, he holds up a roast chicken.

As the scene continues, we learn much more about Janos through his dialogue. The man is definitely an "original," attempting to live by his own standards—a fact which becomes more baffling to the very conservative Joey.

Incidentally, a technical point worth mentioning is the avoidance of *radio* lines in film dialogue. Note when Janos holds up the chicken, he says:

```
            JANOS
    He gave me . . . this!
```

He does *not* say:

```
            JANOS
    He gave me a chicken.
```

The latter is a descriptive line, a hangover from radio drama when it was necessary to make people "see with their ears." While it is essential to do this in radio, it is superfluous in film, since we *see* the chicken. We never point up the obvious.

Most beginning writers are too self-conscious to "talk" their dialogue while they are writing. They sit rigidly at the typewriter, and as the page fills up with words that are pleasing to the eye, they are satisfied. They are forgetting one important thing, however: A speech that may *look* fine on paper may not necessarily *sound* right. These lines in your drama must have another dimension. Unlike words in a novel, the words in a teleplay must be spoken, and, in their context, they must sound natural—*alive.* Here is where your ear and your sense of rhythm come into play. Instinctively, you should have a feel for how long a speech should be—when it should be interrupted, when it should build to fever pitch, and, in contrast, when words should be used very sparingly. All this should be intuitive, and will come naturally, with experience; if the writer becomes absorbed in the scene, the characters will automatically seem to speak their own lines. The trick is to catch the dialogue as it flows from the action. If you can do this at the typewriter, fine. But if you're blocked, then walk away from it. I mean this literally. Go to another part of the room, set your scene, people it in your imagination, and start to improvise. A tape recorder can be enormously helpful at this point.

Here is a sample of dialogue from a teleplay I wrote years ago called *Friends before Freud.* It plays easily. The lines are chosen to suggest comedy, to create a light, bright mood. The character Milly is the key. She is warm, not very bright, completely guileless, and in love with Larry, the protagonist. Larry is one of the rare young men who seem almost too well adjusted in a frenzied world. He is just returning from a business trip and has been treated to a free analysis by his New York taxi driver. Larry opens his apartment door and finds Milly waiting for him:

```
                    MILLY
           Larry!  Hi.

                    LARRY
           Aren't you in the wrong
           apartment?

                    MILLY
           Now, is that a nice way to
```

       talk to your neighbor?
       I'm watering your plants.

She takes his hand and leads him to the
plants.

       Look, you're a father. Two
       new leaves while you were
       gone.

           LARRY
       Milly, you're wonderful.
       How do you do it?

           MILLY
       I talk to them. They like
       me. The whole place likes
       me, even the windows...

She leads him to the windows.

       Notice anything different?

           LARRY
       I can see through them.

Milly looks very pleased with herself.

       Milly, why do you knock
       yourself out?

           MILLY
       It's simple -- because I'm
       a dope. They aren't even
       my windows.

Larry starts to change the subject.

                         LARRY
          Look, what do you say to-

                    MILLY (cuts in)
          Larry, every time you go
          away, it's as if I'm...
          I'm waiting for you to-

                    LARRY (cuts in)
          How about a drink? Why
          don't I whip up some nice
          dry martinis?

                         MILLY
          Relax. They're all whipped.

She opens the door of the portable
refrigerator near the bar of the living
room. She removes a pitcher of drinks,
two chilled glasses and a plate of
canapes. She places them on a tray.

                         LARRY
          Milly, you're a genius!

                         MILLY
          I know. I know.

She follows Larry as he carries the tray
to the coffee table in front of the
couch.

               For all the good it does
               me!

Larry is about to sit down when Milly
stops him.

Look out. Don't sit on
that!

Larry holds up a square of cardboard
which has the words "DEAR LARRY" written
on it.

I didn't finish. I was
going to hang it on the
door.

                    LARRY
"Welcome home?"

                    MILLY
No... I was going to print
LOVE THY NEIGHBOR.

                    LARRY
That's nice.

He sips his drink.

She sidles up to him on the couch.

                    MILLY
It's very serious...
It's in the Bible.
(pause) Love thy
neighbor.

She kisses him lightly. He doesn't
respond.

I wish you were more
religious.

Note the rhythm of the dialogue in this scene. Short, clipped, in keeping with the comedy mood. Read it aloud. Then, for contrast, read some of Janos Miklos' speeches from the father-and-son dialogue preceding it. Can you sense the difference in rhythm?

```
                    JANOS
          Youth is treasure.
          Truth is treasure.
          You are youthful.
          You are the most truth-
          ful boy I know, and as
          you grow, you shine.
```

The speech is read slowly, uninterrupted because Janos is a man who *declaims*. He orates. So the author must supply him with sonorous words.

Milly, on the other hand, has a skittery personality, spirited, playful. Her words must reflect the bubbly character she is. In each case, the words themselves comprise the right rhythm.

Significant silences

As important as dialogue is, there are times when it should be minimized. Often what one *doesn't* say becomes significant. In place of words, a deliberate pause by a character—a purposeful silence—can be extremely telling.

Take the following scene: A husband and wife have quarreled. They have said searing things that hurt each other the night before. Now it is morning.

```
INT. KITCHEN -- MORNING

Anne, holding a coffee cup stands look-
ing out of the window.  Her face is
drawn,tense.  Ben enters.  She turns
```

```
to look at him but says nothing.  Again
she directs her attention to the window.


Ben, very tired, pours himself a cup of
coffee.  He sips it.  He looks pleadingly
toward Anne at the other side of the
room, but he is being ignored.  Finally
he breaks the silence.

                    BEN
          Have you been up long?

She nods.

          I hardly slept at all...
          I was thinking about--


He stops, hoping she'll turn around.
He waits.  She is impassive.

                    BEN
          Anne, listen -- those
          things I said last night
          -- I didn't mean them.
          (another pause)  I was
          half drunk.

Her silence maddens him.  He shouts.

          Anne... I'm talking to you!
```

It is evident that Anne's stillness contributes to the tension of
the scene. Her smoldering anger comes through by her non-re-
sponse. It is frustrating, humiliating to Ben who would welcome
strong words at this point—anything but this lack of communication. Their physical separation—she at the window, he at the table

at the other end of the room—is another revealing factor which adds to the strained atmosphere.

In the same vein, another type of dialogue effective in such scenes is what I call *Counterpoint Dialogue*. Let's consider the same passage, but this time with one change. See what happens (in the latter part of the scene) when we substitute irrelevant speeches for Anne's silence. Note how her words follow a train of thought despite Ben's interruptions.

                    BEN
          Have you been up long?

Anne nods.

          I hardly slept at all...
          I was thinking about--

He stops, hoping she'll turn around.
He waits. She is impassive.

          Anne, listen -- those
          things I said last night...

                    ANNE
          It looks like snow.

                    BEN
          I was half-drunk.

                    ANNE
          Could be a storm.

                    BEN
          I didn't mean them.

                    ANNE
          A blizzard, maybe...

```
        BEN (shouting)
    I'm talking to you!

        ANNE (very quietly)
    I thought you said every-
    thing you had to say ...
    last night.
```

In this example Anne is, again, provoking Ben, not by her silence, but something equally as frustrating. By not talking to him directly, she is totally avoiding the issue at hand. Moreover, she compounds his anger by pursuing her own line of thought which has nothing whatever to do with him at the moment. The more he tries to get to her, to make contact, the more she pushes him away with meaningless words. Used sparingly and in context this Counterpoint Dialogue can be very effective.

Still another variation on this theme is something called *Double Dialogue*. Briefly, it is dialogue on two levels:

1. Words spoken superficially—the let's-make-conversation type. These are used concurrently with:

2. The non-spoken words; the camera conveys a deeper, more personal "dialogue" between two people that is shown visually, but not verbalized.

In the classic film *Brief Encounter*, recently remade for television, there's an absorbing scene in which the two middle-aged people suddenly recognize their deep love for each other. It is never spoken. They sit opposite each other in a lean-to, sheltered from a sudden storm. As they drink their tea, they converse. The man, a doctor, is talking about his medical research. The woman asks pertinent questions about lung disease, and he answers them. This is all happening on a *surface* level. But on a deeper level, the camera comes in to show us the sudden recognition of an intense love between them. Their eyes lock; their faces express tenderness.

We can almost hear the words *I love you* on a subliminal level. It's as if we, the viewers, provide the unspoken dialogue, prompted by the intimate, sensitive camera that reveals the inner feelings of these people.

The camera's "voice"

There are some scenes in which dialogue should not only be minimized, but cut entirely. Again, the camera is so revealing that it can often "speak" far more effectively than the actors. A look, a gesture, a pause can be significant. Words, even well-chosen words, can sometimes clutter a scene when there is no need for them. When we are expressing grief, rage, joy, love—we are usually so "choked up," it is difficult to verbalize our feelings. Certainly this is true in drama. Take, for example, an unforgettable moment in a film called *A Man and a Woman*. It is late afternoon. The man is alone on the beach, waiting, afraid even to hope that the woman will meet him there. Then suddenly he sees her coming toward him. They run to each other and embrace and he picks her up and twirls her around, joyfully. A dog, caught up in the rhythm of the dance-like scene, twirls too as if he is a happy extension of their joy. . . . *Not a word is spoken.* The insistent surf beating against the shore is sound enough, beautifully in rhythm with the flow of the scene.

Silence between two people can denote *conflict* as well as joy. An excellent example is in a teleplay called *Double Solitaire*, by Robert Anderson. Here the author uses moments of silence to point up frustration and lack of communication between his two major characters, a couple whose marriage is breaking up. In a desperate attempt to revive their old feeling for each other, the husband suggests a holiday on a deserted beach. They are alone together, but they are still estranged—especially the wife, who is unable to respond to her husband's affection. It is too late. She has been hurt too much to make a fresh start, and we see this futility in her face, her gestures. At the same time, in her husband we see the growing apprehension, the frustration. We know the break in the marriage is irreparable.

Another revealing example of conflict in a non-verbal scene is in Kay Fanin's sensitive teleplay, *Tell Me Where It Hurts*. In preparing for bed, the middle-aged wife takes a new nightgown out of its wrapping and shows it to her husband who is already in bed. His only response is a tired grunt. He is exhausted and quickly falls into a heavy sleep. The wife, resigned, sadly places the nightgown in her dresser drawer and closes it slowly. The gesture is symbolic of what she feels about herself: shut out. Non-existent. Useless.

XII

OUTLINE
AND BREAKDOWN

IN THE early days of television, a writer was one of the most vulnerable people in the profession. Young, anxious to break into the new medium, he would spend days writing an entire script on speculation, grateful for the chance of submitting it to a producer.

It was not unusual for the producer to suggest changes in the script and for the writer to comply willingly. Although such changes meant considerable rewriting, the playwright rarely mentioned money for this work: To the writer, the prospect of a *final sale* was enough incentive to work.

I know of an instance in which a play, rewritten to conform to the producer's ideas, was submitted again and praised warmly; but before it was actually bought, a few more changes were suggested. By the time the *third* revision was presented, the entire series was suddenly cancelled. The writer was stranded. Not having been paid for his efforts up to that point, he had nothing to show for his investment of time and creative energy. All he could do was to chalk it up to experience.

In all fairness, we must keep in mind that at the time television was a new, untried medium in which everyone was groping, experimenting, learning. And if exploitation was prevalent, it was part of the growing process. True, there were no set rules, no "constitution" to govern the newcomers, but as the industry grew at a fantastic rate, it became evident that guidelines for the protection of writers were a necessity.

In 1953 television writers were admitted into the Screen Writers Guild which, at that point, changed its name to the Writers Guild of America. At long last, television writers had a protective umbrella. The Guild quickly established rules for the profession; among the many "shall nots" was one pertaining to the submission of scripts. No longer could a writer be *asked* to do a script on speculation. However, he may voluntarily submit a one-page outline—a story line of the play he has in mind. If the producer finds it promising, the writer is called in to confer on the material. Then follows a step-by-step assignment in which the writer is paid as he writes, first for the breakdown, which is a scene-by-scene plan of the teleplay, then for the first draft, and finally for the completed, polished script. If the producer is not happy with the way the work is progressing, he can at any stage dismiss the writer, as long as he pays for the work done up to that point. Incidentally, this rarely happens. Once the outline is accepted, the professional writer usually sees the play to its conclusion.

It follows that the outline (or story line) is the crucial factor in this process—the one chance for the writer to impress the buyer with his ability and to open the door to a possible sale.

OUTLINE

What constitutes a good outline? It must convey the salient facts of the script you have in mind. Succinctly, it tells the plot, describes the essential characters, and sets the general mood of the play. It is always written in the third person, present tense.

The beginning of your outline should immediately catch the reader's interest. Much as in a drama, the essential conflict should start as soon as possible. As the plot unwinds, the reader should sense the mounting *progression* of the scenes and be drawn to the characters as well.

Here are the opening paragraphs of an outline by Hector Troy for his teleplay, *Where's My Little Gloria?*

After a tour in Vietnam, Eddie Maldonado returns to his home in the heart of Spanish Harlem, New York, only to discover that his sister has died of an overdose of heroin at her high school.

Distraught over her death, he seeks out the pusher and beats him mercilessly, almost killing him.

Frankie, his younger brother, admonishes him for such a stupid and reckless act, arguing that "people bigger than God are calling the shots," and it would be futile and dangerous to pursue the matter. A few days later, Eddie accidentally discovers that Frankie (for all his big talk) is dealing in drugs. Outraged, Eddie accuses him of Gloria's death.

Note how the author, in his first sentence, gets the play off the ground. Each succeeding sentence carries the plot forward. At the same time, the reader is caught up with the relationship of the brothers and the very strong conflict that develops. Note, too, the lack of lengthy descriptions. Because of the space limitation, the author confines himself to "what is happening," but oddly enough, the emotional content is not sacrificed. Woven deftly into the plot line, the characters and their strong feelings come through.

In a different vein, here is the completed outline of a science-fiction teleplay, *Minus One* by Wendy Friedman.

The year is 2037 A.D. Pax. The world is quiet, frictionless, harmonious. Unending peace is assured by means of a medical technique that removes the brain cells that relate to violent emotions. Hate. Anger. Love.

Taz Dunlap is the last citizen to undergo this simple procedure. Recovery is swift and he is soon back at his normal routine, which is working at the Architectural Complex.

Taz, however, soon begins to feel twinges of emotion. Anger. Slivers of guilt or competitiveness. In an emotionless world, he tries to hide this side of his humanity which seems to have survived.

Preparations, meanwhile, are being made for the third annual Uni-World Celebration. All branches of the society are working on different projects for this spectacle.

Taz's design has been one of those chosen and he throws his energy and emotions into its creation. Feeling checked and watched at every level, he has no one to turn to. Until he meets Jutta, a young woman who, although seeming to fit society's emotionless norms, nevertheless seems to Taz to be more "human." An attachment develops between them, blossoming into love for Taz and into an almost-love for Jutta, who still cannot feel what he can.

Learning the worst, that he is to go into "corrective" therapy which would turn him into an automaton, Taz chooses destruction along with his creation rather than to submit to an inhuman society. Knowing why he chose to die, and witnessing it, finally breaks Jutta's already pierced emotional barrier. She begins to become a living, feeling human being.

Contrary to the rule of starting with conflict, the author in the preceding outline uses her first two paragraphs to set the mood—the way-out atmosphere of the play. Because of its science-fiction nature, this is not only permissible, it is necessary. In this case, the unique setting must be described before the plot line is revealed. But note how adroitly the author handles the opening. The terse style. The cold, dispassionate tone: "The world is quiet, frictionless, harmonious." In six paragraphs, the author has written a complete story line that contains all the essential components of an intriguing, well-constructed play.

Economy of words

Since economy of words is imperative in the writing of outlines, how does one handle character descriptions that are vital to the play?

Here is one answer in the opening paragraphs of the outline of *My Father Talks to Statues*, discussed in the preceding chapter.

To the school authorities, Joey Miklos' father Janos is a man of mystery. He never shows up at any of the school functions. Joey's teacher, Edna Holland, is sorry for Joey, imagining that he is neglected at home.

What she *doesn't* know is that nine-year-old Joey is deliberately keeping his father away because he is ashamed of this booming, bearded, larger-than-life sculptor who is so very different from "normal" fathers.

Again, let me point out that space limitation prohibits lengthy descriptions. Even if this were not true, starting with description would be dull:

Janos Miklos is a tall, bearded, larger-than-life person in every way . . .

How much more interesting to see Janos through his *son's* eyes:

Joey is ashamed of this booming, bearded, larger-than-life sculptor who is so different from "normal" fathers.

The word *ashamed* is the keynote here. It denotes an emotion, the actual pivotal force of the play. It is *because* Joey feels this way that conflict is established. To carry it further, the conflict prevails because of the unique character of Janos. The description, therefore, is woven into the action of the story.

This writing style for an outline is acceptable not only for an original television drama, but for a single episode in a TV series as well. If we were to think up a story line for a *Bonanza* episode (the series is officially ended, but it is often rerun; in any case, it serves as a good example), the outline could start this way:

Ben Cartwright doesn't know what, but there's something about the new hired hand, Josh, he doesn't trust. Ben can forgive his lying about his age—he's sixteen, not nineteen—because he needs the job so desperately, but there's something about him—a sullenness—that Ben finds disturbing. After two days on the ranch, Ben predicts trouble with Josh, but Little Joe doesn't agree with him.

Note that Ben and Little Joe are not described at all. They are continuing characters in the series and don't need to be described. Here, as in an outline for original drama, the story content is most important.

BREAKDOWN

When an editor approves of your outline, he calls you in to discuss the next step: the *Breakdown*. This is a welcome word to a writer. It implies a commitment from the editor to pay for the work. The outline, you remember, is a *voluntary* submission, but from this point on, it is pay-as-you-go. Naturally, this is very conducive to writing. How gratifying to be paid for the preparatory steps which one must do anyway!

For a definition of the breakdown in this context, I like the word *dissection* which is "to divide into separate parts for examination. To analyze." This is precisely what we do when we write a breakdown. We divide the story line into separate parts—that is, into the individual scenes that comprise the play. In doing this scene-by-scene plan of our drama, we are shaping—marking out a course for our completed work.

Unlike the outline, which requires good prose, a breakdown is written in short, almost telegraphic phrases. Words convey the *action* of the play: what happens—where it happens—to whom it happens. There is no description of sets and characters. Rarely is dialogue included. What is important here is the scene-by-scene progression, the inherent conflict, and the dramatic tension that builds to the conclusion of the play. . . . A breakdown, then, is the skeleton, the bare bones that can be examined, analyzed, and finally approved by the editor.

A good breakdown requires a great deal of thought, imagination, and planning. This is where everything you have learned about dramatic construction comes into play. It helps enormously to visualize your characters on an imaginary television screen, to see them in situations, to hear them talk. If you have kept a blueprint (the creative diary we discussed in an earlier chapter), then most of your preliminary work has already been done. By this time you know your characters, your plot, your theme. Now you need to fill in the "sketch" so that the design of the play comes through.

Let's go back to the script of *My Father Talks to Statues*, the play about the boy who is ashamed of his father, and see how the beginning of a breakdown looks on paper.

```
1.   INT. BASEMENT -- NIGHT

     Joey is cooking supper on hot plate in
     corner of studio.  Looks at hopeless
     clutter of statues -- clears off small
     table and sets it.

     Janos enters, smells something burning,
     but he doesn't care.  He brings flowers
     and a chicken, says he's bartered art
     work.  Janos asks Joey about school.
     Joey's evasive.  Janos wants to meet
     teacher -- don't they have an Open
     School Week?  Joey, flustered, lies --
     never!  Janos says it doesn't matter.
     He's sure Joey is the best in the class.
     Joey looks uneasy.

2.   INT. SCHOOL ROOM -- DAY

     Big poster on wall announcing Open School
     Week ... Joey looks at it as the class
     bell rings and he walks toward the exit
     with his friend, Kenney.  At door,
     teacher, Miss Holland calls Joey --
     wants to see him a minute.  Kenney says
     he'll meet him outside.

     Teacher asks Joey if his father is
     planning to come to Open School Week.
     Joey, nervous, makes excuses.  Father
```

```
is very busy -- away at conferences a
lot -- never comes to school -- he's a
very important man.  Teacher wants
father to know how important Joey is --
leader in class, athlete, high marks.
She suggests writing note to father,
urging him to visit.  Joey talks her
out of it -- promises to "persuade"
father, himself.  Mention is made by
Miss Holland about Joey entering the
new Statewide Essay Competition.
Teacher thinks Joey could win if he
works hard at it.
```

And so it goes. Scene follows scene, advancing the action to the end of the play. There is no time or space limitation in the writing of a breakdown. The material dictates the length. Again, let me remind you to state only the essential action. And *only what can be seen on the screen.* For example, it is perfectly permissible for us to suggest Joey's frustration as he looks at the clutter of the statues. This can be seen on the screen by Joey's facial expression. We actually see him trying to make some semblance of order. He has to clear the table in order to set it for supper. Therefore, when we state that "Joey looks at hopeless clutter of statues," in the word *hopeless,* we are already implying his frustration.

However, it would be *wrong* to write:

> Joey looks at hopeless clutter of statues and thinks how nice it would be if he lived in a real apartment—a clean, ordered one in which everything has its place.

As stated, all this is in Joey's mind and means nothing to the viewer. We cannot know what he is thinking specifically. As we mentioned before, an expression is one thing. It can be portrayed by an actor. But his thoughts are part of an "inner" description and have no place in a teleplay. Even in a breakdown, this should be checked. A good craftsman writes only what can be seen on the screen.

To take it a step further, if we wanted to show what Joey is actually thinking, this could easily be done by an *Insert*—a flash of a scene that portrays Joey's thought visually—in this case, a well-ordered living room. This is the way we designate the Insert:

```
INSERT -- INT. LIVING ROOM -- DAY

The room is a charming, modern,
uncluttered living room, comfortably
furnished.

BACK TO:

INT. STUDIO BASEMENT -- NIGHT

Joey clears table and sets it.
```

This Insert is a visualization of Joey's thoughts. Used sparingly and only when necessary, Inserts can be very effective.

TREATMENT

Many people confuse the word *treatment* with *outline*. They are not synonymous. An outline is a one-page plot account of a television play.

A treatment, on the other hand, is a detailed, expertly written story for motion pictures. The television writer need not concern himself with this form. Actually, it is obsolete even in motion picture writing. Today, film producers prefer to see finished screenplays.

XIII

MARKETS

"HOW MUCH do they pay for television scripts?" Beginners invariably ask this question and they have a right to know what the profession offers in terms of payment.

The money for television writing is good. Naturally, there are some variables depending on the type of program, the time-slot (daytime drama or prime-time evening), and the length of the drama (half-hour, hour, hour-and-a-half, or two hours). Roughly, payments range from over three thousand dollars for a half-hour show to the nine-thousand-dollar bracket for a ninety-minute show. A film for television can bring the writer over eleven thousand dollars. Then there are the residuals. For an hour-long rerun, the payment is two thousand dollars. There are also minimums in the pay TV and cassette fields, and the Writers Guild of America contract covers the writer who works with any other compact device that is now on the market or on the drawing boards for the future.

From the above, no one can dispute that the writer is well-paid for his efforts. Realistically, however, the competition is keen, and the breakthrough, especially for a new writer, is difficult. Even for the experienced writer, the profession is a precarious one. Because of the nature of the business, nothing is certain. A show may be successful one season and be a disaster the next. Since television has a mass audience, it must make an effort to please the taste of the majority. Sponsors rely upon the ratings to determine what that taste is.

In examining the complex subject of markets, it is interesting to look back and trace the trends beginning with the so-called Golden Age of television in the fifties, when drama came to us "live from New York." In those days, a free-lance writer had an incredible market. Half-hour and hour dramatic shows were presented "live" every night of the week. Kraft Theatre, Studio One, Lux Video Theatre, Playhouse Ninety and so many more were open to the new television dramatist who was anxious to make his mark in the field. And many did. Talented young aspirants became seasoned professionals—writers like Tad Mosel, Horton Foote, Rod Serling, Paddy Chayefsky sprang into prominence as they contributed steadily to the burgeoning market. New York was the ideal place to perfect their craft.

But gradually the phrase, "live from New York," gave way to a new phrase, "filmed in Hollywood." Because of rising costs, it was economically sound to make Hollywood the new television center, and the weather there was conducive to outdoor shooting. With the demise of the giant movie complexes, motion picture lots were idle, waiting to be used, as were the unemployed craftsmen.

How did all this affect the writer? As the New York market dried up, many television writers moved to California and made the transition from "live" to "film." For them, new opportunities opened as new types of shows were presented.

If a Western series is tried out and becomes a hit, a rash of Westerns soon follows. Television is imitative, constantly hoping to latch onto a successful formula. Situation comedies followed. "The audience wants continuity," said the network officials. "They want the same characters but different situations week after week." And they got them! At this writing, they are still getting them—some excellent, others mediocre, but the "sitcom" (as it is known in the industry) is a flourishing format. Doctor shows are also popular, and until we run out of diseases, these programs will probably go on and on. The past few seasons, cops-and-robbers have been rampant on the television screen. The chase is exciting, and "get that car" is the key phrase. Jeopardy, mystery, suspense, ghost stories all find their way into prime time.

Then, curiously enough, a series about a mountain family made its debut. *The Waltons* featured the old-fashioned values— warmth, love of a family struggling to survive in the depression era. No one in the industry expected it to make the slightest ripple in the ratings. But they were wrong. *The Waltons* appealed to millions of people and immediately produced imitators.

From this "history," we can only conclude that television is unpredictable. No one can foretell the success of a new project. This is unsettling, of course, but the *unexpected* is a way of life in the television industry. It took enormous courage to go against the trend and launch new types of programs like *The Waltons* and *All in the Family*. If they had failed, the network executives would have been blamed for bad judgment. Certainly it is safer not to experiment, but how prosaic and unexciting television is when it is merely imitative. Fortunately, in spite of the banality, there are always innovators who are willing to take a chance on the new, the untried concept in the hope that some indefinable factor will appeal to an audience. Since television is a constantly changing medium, it must always be receptive to new and vital concepts— which means *growing*.

And you, the writer, must grow with it. This is why I strongly advocate that aspiring television writers begin by learning their craft. Even if the market seems closed, who can predict the new opportunities that may be waiting for you in the future?

Right now, for example, the pendulum is swinging back to original drama—not as it was years ago with many dramatic anthology shows featured every night of the week. But there is the occasional Special which stresses noteworthy plays and fine acting. On a non-regular basis, there is the Hallmark Theatre or the General Electric Theatre that offer us outstanding entertainment. In addition, there are movies written especially for television and shown by the major networks on prime time. Some of our recent award-winning dramas have come from this category: plays like Paul Junger Witt's *Brian's Song*, and Roger Gimbel's television dramatization of Margaret Craven's best-selling novel, *I Heard the Owl Call My Name.*

In daytime programming, one of the networks, ABC, has occasionally interrupted its regularly scheduled programs in order to present a ninety-minute drama to its daytime viewers.

Does this mean a resurgence of drama in the future? Possibly. No one can tell. And if more plays are bought in the future, what are the chances for the newcomer to break into the medium?

Here is the dichotomy: On one hand, television devours material at a fantastic rate and sorely needs fresh new talent to refurbish it. On the other hand, a hectic schedule plus the fear of working with a new or untried writer deter the network executive from opening his door to the novice.

How to *get that door open* is the problem facing the unseasoned writer. It is difficult but not impossible. Here are some of the ways.

AGENTS

You may or may not like the idea of an agent, but it's an indisputable fact that the agent is a vital part of the television world. To paraphrase an old saying, he's "the shortest distance between the writer and the editor." A really good agent can save you hours of hunting for open markets. Often he can act as a sounding board, brief you on the format of a new show, introduce you and your work to the proper executives. He can negotiate for you, sometimes asking a far better price than you would have dared to ask. If he is truly competent, he will judge your potential as well as your present ability, and as you grow in stature, he will guide you by selecting the assignments that will advance your career.

In spite of these pluses, there may be those of you who object to the idea of agents. What's the alternative? To submit your material directly to the network. You must know, however, that your script will form a part of a mountain of unsolicited scripts—mostly written by amateurs. Will it be read? Eventually, provided you submit a standard release form (which you send for before submission) which states that your work is original and that the company is not liable for any damages that may be payable in the case of libel or plagiarism suits. Here again, a writer may balk, but in all fairness, much of the "slush" material comes from people who have creative ideas but very little knowledge of script writing technique.

On the other hand, what about the legitimate writer's protection? How can you be sure your idea won't be stolen? Unfortunately, an idea or even an outline cannot be copyrighted. Only a full play is acceptable for copyright at the Register of Copyrights, Washington, D.C. However, you can send a copy of your script to yourself by *registered mail*. When it arrives, do not open the envelope. The postmark date and your receipt of registration could possibly be the evidence needed to prove that you wrote the material prior to the time it (or a portion of it) was actually used on the air. It would help to keep records of the dates that you sent the material to the producer and the correspondence between you that followed.

On the whole, people in the industry are honest. The unscrupulous person who lifts an idea or a bit of dialogue is a *rarity*. In any event, if you are always apprehensive of submitting material, you will never feel comfortable in the medium. It also helps to understand that ideas are sometimes in the "collective air." With so many writers thinking creatively, there's bound to be duplication.

Coming back to the submission of unsolicited material, you may have to wait a very long time to get your work read. In some cases, the market can actually close before your work is evaluated. This is not because the network readers are lax. On the contrary. They do the best they can to wade through mountains of material—most of it hopelessly inadequate and unprofessional.

This is why an editor prefers to work with agents. When a

manuscript is brought in by an agent, the editor knows it has been screened, and in another person's opinion, at least, it has merit. Again, a good agent builds his reputation on submitting good work. His judgment should be sound, and though perhaps he isn't right all of the time, he bats a fine average. Your work, therefore, submitted by an agent, gets you out of the "slush pile" and into a category far more worthy of consideration.

It comes down to this, then: *How to get an agent.* Let's analyze the situation from two points of view: the writer's and the agent's.

The writer's "case"

You are a newcomer. You have never had anything produced. But you are convinced you have ability, and what is just as important, you have taken the time to study your craft. You know television technique and format. You know what a play is. And you know, given a chance, you can develop into a professional writer. You have several full-length scripts in your portfolio to prove it.

The agent's side

The agent is a professional. He knows the trends—what's "in" this season—what's on its way out. He has access to the right people—the ones who read and evaluate scripts for possible sale. He wants to make a sale, naturally, in order to collect his commission. His commodity is creative material.

But he cannot make a living (nor can the writer) with the sale of one script. An agent looks for a writer who is not only proficient, but prolific as well. After the first sale, he wants to know if there's another idea brewing. Are you imaginative, disciplined, productive? Farseeing, he is thinking of the future as well as the present. Perhaps he discovers you have a talent for prose. He is aware that another route to a movie sale, for example, is through the printed page. Editors, in their search for screen material, are constantly combing magazines and published novels. Well-written prose can be the stepping-stone to the screenplay you have in mind. If your novel or short story has cinematic possibilities, there's a good chance that with the proper representation, it will be bought for the screen. But to be "properly represented" you, the writer, must first impress the agent with your ability.

Contacting the agent

This is not easy, but it can be done. It takes patience, persistence, and a strong belief in yourself.

In your search for an agent, you'll find that the two best areas are the production centers: Hollywood and New York. If you live in or near these cities, you'll find the names of literary agents in the classified phone directory. Even if you live a long distance from either coast, you can still obtain an out-of-town directory and make note of addresses and phone numbers of these agents. But don't stop here. Go to the library and look for issues of writers' magazines that have featured articles on television writing and markets. In them you're bound to find names of recommended agents. Another source is a small publication called *Ross Reports*. This is an excellent source of television production information for the east and west coasts—network and syndicated projects—as well as major local programs. In each monthly issue there is a list of agents handling television scripts. It is published by Television Index, Inc., 150 Fifth Avenue, New York, New York 10011. Individual copies are available for a nominal charge.

Armed with more than enough names, study your lists. You will find that some agents are open to new writers. Others have a small, select roster and want to keep it that way. Concentrate on the first category. There are several methods of approach:

1. Write a short, compelling letter that you hope will cause the agent to invite you to submit your material. I say short because an

agent has no time to wade through pages of your autobiography no matter how fascinating your life may be. It is best to tell him briefly who you are, what you have in the way of written material, and why you think your work will interest him. This, incidentally, is the time-tested rule of writing to any potential employer: How can you benefit *him?*

2. You can send one script directly to the agent with a short covering letter telling him about yourself. Including a stamped, self-addressed envelope is mandatory and usually assures you a reply.

3. The personal touch is very helpful. If you know someone who knows a good agent, ask to be recommended. This is, of course, the best method. Agents, like network editors, are barraged by material, and you naturally stand a better chance of being noticed through a personal introduction.

4. Try to have your work produced locally before you submit a script. I realize this is not always possible, but it is an excellent method of getting attention. A local television station can be a good proving ground for the beginner, provided it has the facility for producing work by new talent. Too often, however, the budgets don't allow for local dramatic productions. In this case, it would be wise to rewrite your play for the stage. Perhaps you can arrange to have it done by a little theatre group, a college drama class, somewhere that allows you to see your play performed. If you feel it is of professional caliber, let the agent know about it. Send him a printed program, or better still, if feasible, invite him or her to see your play. I know several writers who were "picked up" by agents in just such a manner—and they are now actively writing for television.

When you finally come to terms with an agent, it is only right to let him represent you exclusively for whatever time you and he agree on. But don't be too hasty to sign a long-term contract with the agent of your choice. In the beginning, it is wise for you both to work on a pleasant but cautious basis. Assuming he likes your work and sells your script, he will receive a ten percent commission. He will, of course, urge you to write more. Gradually, as you get to know each other, you will see how you get on professionally. Before you commit yourself legally with a long-term contract, be certain he is the agent you want to represent you in the future. A good working relationship is vitally important.

XIV

WRITER'S CHECKLIST

UP TO this point, we have analyzed, explored, and studied the anatomy of dramatic construction of a television play. In the next part of the book we demonstrate how all these elements and techniques come together in a television play from the beginning of the idea to the finished script.

But before we trace this development, there are still threads to be tied, lists to be checked, seemingly small or minor points to take note of that may on the surface seem unimportant—and yet, in the overall scheme of a writer's world, I think they are significant. *Discipline, attitude,* and *persistence* play a notable part in your career.

Discipline

Talent and technique mean nothing if a writer cannot bring himself to work. At the beginning of a project, especially, it seems that everything conspires to keep the playwright away from the typewriter. Lethargy takes over, then procrastination, then guilt, self-hate, and further lethargy.

In most cases, the underlying enemy is fear of committing oneself. It is so much easier to *talk a script* than to write it. You can experience the same glow that comes with creativity, but because it is not down on paper, it is safe—*fail safe.*

The truth is, it takes courage and a certain amount of ego to put words on paper. The ego assures you the words are important enough to be read and eventually played. Courage is needed to plunge in, take the chance, make the commitment, and if the urge to write is strong enough, once you start, the writing will come more easily.

If you still have trouble, then discipline yourself with short-term promises. Promise to get to the typewriter at a certain hour. Experiment at first to discover your best writing time. Are you an early riser? Do you think more creatively in the morning? Or do you really come to life later on in the day? Do you find the evening hours more conducive to work? Once you've established a writing time, stick to it. Promise yourself you will sit at your desk for one hour. If you're a morning person, that hour may be *before* you start your day at the office. The primary thing is to be at your typewriter at the same time every day. At first, perhaps, you will write nothing. Your mind will be a blank. Let it. Sit there the following day. And the day after that. Establish a new habit. You will find that gradually the words will come and your attention span will be far greater than you had ever imagined. Soon you'll be caught up in the joy, the exhilaration of putting words on paper, and eventually going to the typewriter will become automatic.

When your writing is finished for the day, leave your desk with a good feeling. Don't consciously work on your script when your brain is tired. Relax, knowing that you've put in a good hour (or two) and that you'll be ready for another productive day tomorrow. Naturally, as the play progresses, you will want to find extra hours to devote to it. Only you can pace yourself. The important thing is getting started.

If you are ever to become a serious writer, this discipline is absolutely essential, especially in television. The profession is governed by hours and minutes and seconds. Deadlines are a way of life. If, for example, you are given three weeks to complete a first draft, that script is expected on a specific date. There is no time to be self-indulgent—to wait for inspiration. Only day-by-day writing on a self-imposed schedule will produce the finished product on time.

Attitude

In the fifties a professional television writer could sit at his desk for a month and produce a play for one of the many dramatic anthology programs on the air at that time. His agent would sell the script, sometimes on the first try. Soon afterward, a contract and check would be in the mail. Often, he would be asked to the rehearsal of his play, but in some cases he would *not* be invited. In fact, there was a time in the industry when directors were adamant about the "No Visitors" rule, which applied to writers as well as to the general public. Writers had on occasion proved troublesome, and as a result, they had virtually no contact with the people who produced their material.

This is not true today. Because of the Guild rulings, writers work very closely with television script editors. Once the story line is approved, the author is called in to do the breakdown. Possible changes, character development, budget restrictions—all these topics are discussed in the editor's office. It is at these meetings that the writer's attitude is of utmost importance. If he is belligerent, unable to listen, arrogant, he will be killing his chances of working in the future, not only with this particular editor but with others as well. Word travels fast in television, and reputations, good and bad, are quickly established.

Most writers realize that television is a people-oriented medium. It depends not on one but on many craftsmen. Although the script is vitally important, the writer must also have the proper perspective of himself in relation to these craftsmen. These are the people who make his words come alive. Mutual respect is imperative. The ideal writer is cooperative and aware of the overall problems. He has the ability to listen and to keep an open mind, and is capable of working under pressure when last-minute script changes are needed. There is so much legitimate tension in the mechanical aspects of a production, there is no room for temperament.

This does not negate the writer's privilege of speaking up for what he thinks is right. Certainly if he objects to a change, he has every right to state his feelings. It's the *way* he states his case that creates the right or the wrong impression. If he is articulate and persuasive, he may win his point. But he'll never win if he becomes defensive and belligerent. I have seen good writers lose assignments because they are, to quote an editor, "Trouble." Keep in mind that editors have to adhere to certain regulations set by their superiors. They don't make the policy of the program; their job is to carry it through. Like the writer, they want the best possible script, and sometimes their reasons for buying or rejecting an idea are not apparent to one unfamiliar with the inner workings of the network.

Persistence

There is no magic formula to help one become a professional in television writing—or in any other field of writing, for that matter. Even when you have all the necessary qualities for success—talent, ambition, craftsmanship—you still need that "little bit of luck," a chance acquaintance in the field, being in the right place at the right time. But if luck is elusive, a reservoir of persistence is essential. If you truly believe you have ability, you must be tenacious. In spite of rebuffs, continue to write and improve your craft. If drama is your forte, create it, even if there is no market for it at the time. Remember that television is changeable. Tastes change; a new season can offer new types of programs and fresh opportunities.

No one can stop you from writing. A regular job should not

deter you. An hour of writing before you go to work or when you get home can keep the creative juices flowing.

In spite of rejection, disappointment, frustration, the true writer will not give up. As a matter of fact, he cannot. To this type of person, writing is a way of life as natural as breathing.

If you are one of these people impelled to put words on paper, and if there is joy in the output, then by all means, continue to do so. If nothing else, you'll become more facile and your work will improve, and, it is hoped, so will your chances of becoming successful.

Persistence has paid off handsomely for so many writers who, after their first achievement were heralded by the critics as "overnight sensations." *Overnight* means years, perhaps, of dogged determination to keep writing.

Part Two

DEMONSTRATION

Diary of a Television Play

XV
DIARY OF A
TELEVISION PLAY

IN THE first part of this book, we analyzed the various elements of dramatic construction and, wherever possible, have given examples to illustrate a point.

But elements of themselves do not make a TV drama. Just as the individual instruments of an orchestra need to be brought together to create specific music, the components of a play must be carefully coordinated to form an entity.

To show how this works, we are going to trace a full-length television script from its inception and touch on all the preliminary steps that led up to the actual writing—i.e., the blueprint, the outline, and the breakdown. In other words, we are going behind the scenes in an effort to reveal the creative process at work. Certainly it is an elusive process, operating differently in each individual. Nevertheless, it may prove helpful to see it on paper.

For several reasons I have chosen a television play of my own called *A Door You Can Close*, a nostalgic piece set in the early fifties. For one thing, it is a half-hour drama and can be dissected easily for the purpose of demonstrating dramatic technique. For another, it is a play that sprang from a strong conviction and emerged almost full-blown as soon as I perceived the theme.

Here then is the *diary* of a dramatic script. In the step-by-step process that follows, it is my hope that this Demonstration will serve as a guideline.

If you refer back to the chapter on *Blueprint*, you will note that it is the personal scribblings of creative ideas, not necessarily in sequence that eventually emerges as the *backbone* of your play. The blueprint is for you alone. It is as personal, as private, as a diary.

BLUEPRINT

On way back from drive to see leaves turning, H. and I dropped in on old friend of H.'s mother—lives in Rockaway Beach. . . . Mrs. G., in late forties, runs a rooming house a block from the beach . . . said she just sold the house and is moving to Brooklyn to live with a widow like herself—old friend of the family's. Mrs. G. is thin, wiry—pinched mouth—hard facial lines—hands rough as if she has done housework all of her life.

She showed us around the place—community kitchen, living room, front porch—everything very dowdy—rooms on first and second floors—letters and numbers, ex:— 1A—2B, etc.

Saw picture of little girl—about ten—nice, sensitive face—Mrs. G.'s only child—grown up now, married, has children of her own.

I'm intrigued. I asked questions: Did she grow up here in the rooming house? Yes, said her mother. Did she have one of these rooms? No. The little girl slept on the couch in the living room.

The line stunned me! It flashed on and off in my head—all during the visit . . . "Slept on the Couch in the Living Room."

I keep seeing the child living in an atmosphere of strangers—there's no *door* in the living room—people come and go—a girl is sleeping on the couch—with all her possessions, maybe, in a cardboard box at the foot of it.

Later that night: I can't sleep. I'm obsessed with the picture of this child. I feel so strongly about this: *a person needs privacy,* especially when she's growing up. . . . Is this a beginning—privacy? . . . Not yet a theme but a direction. Privacy leads to . . . what?

What happens to this girl? I must make her older in my script so that she can eventually leave and find a room of her own. With a door she can close. That's it. The title. *A Door You Can Close.* She's in her late teens, nineteen. Bright. Pretty—more than surface prettiness. Depth. Not going to college . . . Mother wants her to help in the rooming house. Eventually, she will inherit it.

What does the girl want desperately? A room of her own. Who is opposing the want? Her mother. Protagonist: Girl. Ginny—Ginny Harris. Antagonist: Mother—

I must change the locale. California—all-year-round rooming house. Palm tree out front—one of those ordinary places near the beach, rarely has a vacancy during the year.

Theme: Need for privacy leads to independence. . . . That's it. Ginny has a tremendous need for privacy. She must have it to grow. Eventually she grows strong enough to leave her mother and find a place of her own. . . . Independence.

I can see the last scene—the resolution—no dialogue. She walks into another room in another rooming house a few blocks away. She *rents* her *own* room. She closes the door. Puts her plant on the windowsill. It—and she (plant symbol of her)—are finally at home. . . . Introduce plant in first act, maybe in Ginny's entrance, symbol of her homelessness.

Do I have *conflict?* Yes! Ginny wants a room—mother opposes the idea. Why? Because mother is frugal. Frightened. Insecure . . . work on "biography" of mother to find out why she is all these things. Conflict grows. Mother wants to keep Ginny with her—motives are good—she wants to give Ginny security for a "rainy day." That's why she saves every penny. But Ginny wants a different kind of security now. She needs it now—no understanding between them. Can't communicate.

What about *crisis?* What is the turning point? Maybe Ginny is promised a room in the future. Mother is sure there'll never be a vacancy. In order to put Ginny off, mother says something like, "You can have the next room. I promise."

What if the next room becomes vacant unexpectedly—the

largest, the best room in the house. Who lives in it—and how does it become vacant? A retired actress? Maybe. A kind of romantic ex-chorus girl—was in a picture once—never made it. Became a waitress, saved some money, has some stocks—anyhow (work out details in plotting), she leaves, and Ginny moves in. Mother promised her the next vacancy.

Great elation—at last, a room of her own. Play scene in pantomime—Ginny's joy, etc. Then get to crisis:

Ginny comes back to house with two of the roomers. The girls say good night and go to their rooms. Ginny takes her key to open her door. Impossible. The lock's been changed. She panics. Turns on the light in the living room—sees the familiar couch made up as a bed—and her possessions again in the cardboard box at the foot of the couch—the plant sticking out of box. She doesn't believe it.

She crumples up on couch and cries. Now that she's had a taste of her own place, she can't stand the disappointment of being deprived of it. She sobs uncontrollably—angry, frustrated tears. Mother rushes out from the office (she too sleeps on a couch in the office)—she tries to comfort Ginny. Girl is inconsolable.

Climax: After hysteria—Ginny must make up her mind, calmly, resolutely—to take some positive action. Something in her snapped during the crisis. She can't go back—can't be the same again. She makes a decision to leave—gets a typing job and has just enough money to rent a room in an adjoining rooming house.

Scene very touching—climax where she has to tell her mother she is leaving—mother can't understand, is terribly hurt, wants to do the right thing for Ginny—and now she's losing her. Why? Ginny tries to explain—but they speak from two different worlds. Mother can't understand Ginny's basic need for privacy. . . . Mother consumed by desire for security, money. Maybe Ginny says something like: "I'm afraid to stay here—afraid I'll shrivel up. Whatever this money business is, I don't want to catch it" (like a disease).

Resolution: quick scene—in new room—plant on sill—titles over.

What about *Mortar?* It's love. Family ties that kept Ginny from making the decision earlier. She has no malice toward her mother—she knows they're two different people and she has to save herself in order to survive. It is not easy for Ginny to make this move. Essentially, deep down, she *loves* her mother—but she doesn't *like* her. . . . explore the difference.

Get in material about father. How did he influence mother's attitude before his death? What about Ginny's feelings toward him? Is she very much like him? Yes. A dreamer—sensitive. What does she have from her mother? Resoluteness. Determination to survive against all odds. Strength. Do biographies of both characters, and work on plot.

BIOGRAPHIES

Ginny Harris

The morning of Ginny Harris' birth in a San Diego hospital, her father, Tom Harris, was at sea. A merchant marine, he was away a good deal of the time, much to the consternation of his wife, Anne. Though each new sailing was his "last," he couldn't bring himself to live a prosaic life . . . until Ginny was born.

She soon became "Daddy's girl," inheriting his fair coloring, his disarming smile, his fun-loving nature. By contrast, Anne, her mother, was a small brown mouse. Basically a pretty woman, Anne rejected any form of frivolous behavior because of her stern Maine upbringing.

After Ginny was born, Anne finally persuaded Tom to give up the sea, and he was delighted to spend more time with his baby girl. But land jobs were dull, and he drifted from one to another. Being extravagant, he spent the little money he made on presents for Ginny. This angered Anne who was desperately trying to live on a very small budget.

Ginny was four when Tom died of a heart attack. She seemed

inconsolable for months. Anne, as usual, was a pillar of strength. She took the small amount of money she received after his death, borrowed more from her father, and invested it in a small run-down beach rooming house. For as long as Ginny could remember, this was *home* to her. She enjoyed living near the water, but she hated the house itself—the strangers who lived there—her mother's constant catering to them when she, Ginny, needed her, especially in her growing-up years.

Most of all, Ginny hated the penny-pinching. Even when business was good, when all the rooms were occupied (and it looked as if there would never be a vacancy), her mother became more and more frugal, constantly saving for "a rainy day."

Ginny's personality was so contrary to her mother's. There was the love she felt for her, of course, but she sometimes wondered if it was an *obligatory* love. As she grew older, she felt stifled in her mother's presence and resented the lack of communication. A dreamer, an idealist much like her father, Ginny knew her own needs. She reached out for something more than the *basics* that her mother made so important. There was a longing for beauty in Ginny—the sea, music, a flower. These things could stir her, but Anne was unimpressed by her daughter's esthetic nature. The fear of poverty overrode everything.

In her early teens, Ginny began to resent the rooming house more than ever. It was robbing her of her privacy. Sleeping on the living room couch was an assault on her sensitivity.

On her nineteenth birthday, she tried to persuade her mother to let her get a job as a receptionist, but Anne insisted she needed Ginny to help run the rooming house. Every penny she didn't pay out in wages, Anne pointed out, would eventually go to Ginny.

But Ginny needs things *now*—she can't live in the future. And when a small room on the top floor of the house is finally vacant, Ginny pleads with her mother to let her have it!

This is where Ginny is at the opening of the play.

Anne Harris

Anne Harris was born and bred in Maine, the daughter of good, hard-working, thrifty people. A small, wiry child, she was taught to "live plain and have plain ways." There was no coquetry in her, no vanity whatever.

At eleven, she was already working (after school) in her parents' grocery store. There was never too much money, and Anne was taught to save for "a rainy day." Fiercely independent, her parents never wanted to be a burden on their only child when they grew older. They constantly talked of the future and how they had to prepare for it.

In high school, Anne did well at her studies, but socially she was the proverbial wallflower. She was, in her own mind, *plain*, painfully shy, and she made no attempt to use make-up or dress attractively.

But in her early twenties, she became a "late bloomer." Suddenly, she seemed to have all the attributes: a slim figure, shiny auburn hair, large, expressive eyes, and skin glowing with youth. More than this, there was a directness about her, a guilelessness that some young men found very attractive. Anne allowed a person to be himself. She had a talent for listening. She was fragile-looking but strong inside. The combination was intriguing . . . especially to Tom Harris, who recognized in Anne all of the requisites for his ideal wife.

Charmed by his attention, comfortable with him, Anne convinced herself that he had potential for the future.

Though his home base was on the west coast, Tom came to Maine on his holidays, and it wasn't long before he and Anne were engaged. Anne thought she could persuade him to give up the sea and settle down . . . after they were married.

Anne thought wrong. Living ashore, even in San Diego where they moved after a brief honeymoon, was boring to Tom. Time and again he would sign up for one "last" voyage, and Anne would be left alone for months at a time. She was terribly lonely, and her old shyness kept her from making friends easily. California was so different from Maine, and without Tom, she felt strange, displaced.

She found herself wondering if a child would be the anchor to keep Tom home. This time she was right.

After Ginny was born, Tom was happier than he had ever been. He gave up the sea—but he was incapable of keeping a job. Once the challenge was gone, he became restless. He began to drink too much. He was extravagant. The more he spent money, the more frugal Anne became. Frugal and frightened.

The fear of poverty became an obsession with her. . . . What if Tom couldn't provide for her and the child? She wanted Ginny to have a secure future. She had always lived in the future—just as her parents had done. "When Ginny grows up" was her favorite phrase, so much so that she failed to pay attention to the child while she was growing.

When Tom died of a sudden heart attack, a part of Anne died too. She became even more fearful of the future and more determined than ever to care for herself and Ginny, and, like her parents, never to be a burden to her child. Money became her idol—not to enjoy, but to save, to squirrel away. She had to know it was safely in the bank, never to be touched until that "rainy day."

When she first became a widow, she thought of going back to Maine with Ginny, but the prospect of the rooming house intrigued her. She could be independent, live rent free, and, most important, make good steady money all year round.

What she never realized was that the business was robbing her of a chance to be with Ginny, to know her, to grow closer to her as she was growing up. If she were aware of the widening rift between them, it was not on a conscious level. She knew Ginny loved her. How could Anne doubt it when she was doing everything—working night and day—to secure the girl's future! Some day Ginny would realize it and be grateful . . .

This is Anne's thinking when the play opens.

Here is the outline submitted for the script. After approval of the outline, the assignment is given for the Breakdown. As the final step, when the Breakdown has been approved, the writer is commissioned to go to script.

OUTLINE

ROOM FOR RENT . . . nineteen-year-old Ginny Harris never thought she'd see this sign on her mother's beach rooming house in California. The rooms have been occupied for years, and though she finds it very distasteful, Ginny sleeps on the living room couch. What she wants desperately is a room of her own -- a door she can close. But her mother objects. A frugal widow, Mrs. Harris is saving every penny for Ginny's future, unaware of the girl's need to be her own person.

When Ginny pleads for the room and promises to get a job to pay for it, her mother reminds her that she needs her to help in the house. To stop her pleading, she promises her the *next* vacancy, knowing full well it could be in twenty years.

But unexpectedly, it happens in a very short time. The occupant of 2A (the largest room in the house) is a fading actress who suddenly

rekindles her love for her estranged
husband. He is now a doorman in a
posh beach hotel. . . . Ginny,
remembering her mother's promise,
joyfully moves into 2A when Mrs. Nichols
moves out. At last Ginny and her
possessions (which she keeps in a
carton) have a home. Closing the door,
she cannot believe the miracle of
having a room of her own.
      But it's short-lived. When Ginny
comes back from a beach party, she is
locked out of her room, and she's
horrified to see the living room couch
made up as a bed and her carton next
to it. Crumpling on the couch, she
sobs uncontrollably, while her mother
reminds her that some day all the
money from the new tenant will go to
her.
      The following morning Ginny tries
to convince her mother that there are
some things you can't wait for, like
dignity and privacy. She needs these
things *now*, not some day. She hurts
Mrs. Harris, but to survive, Ginny
rents a room for herself in a
neighboring rooming house-- with a door
she can close.

Note:

The script was written for a small budget. I have, therefore, kept
all of the action to *interiors*. For a larger budget and a longer play,
exteriors would have been added, such as: the beach, ext. of swank
hotel, ext. of neighboring rooming house, and several establishing
shots of Southern California. . . . Naturally, exteriors enhance a
script. However, because of the budget limitations, they had to be
implied through the dialogue.

BREAKDOWN

ACT ONE

Hold on sign which reads: "HOLLYWOOD
ARMS -- ROOMS -- VACANCY."

                                 DISSOLVE TO:

INT. COMMUNITY KITCHEN -- MORNING

The kitchen is cluttered with roomers:
Joan and Shirley are looking into the
refrigerator to get something for
breakfast. Bill Miller stands waiting
outside the bathroom door, a towel
slung over his shoulder. ... Mrs.
Harris enters and scolds Yetta, a fat,
good-hearted roomer, for hanging her
bathing suit indoors.

In the midst of all this, Ginny enters,
a shopping bag in one hand, and a small
plant in the other. Mother reminds her
they've a perfectly good palm tree in
the backyard. The plant is an extra-
vagance. Ginny asks if she can rent
the vacant room. She pleads with her
mother -- says she wants it desperately
and will get a job to pay for it. But
mother objects strenuously -- says she
needs Ginny to help run the rooming-
house. They are constantly interrupted
by one boarder or another. Finally,
mother promises Ginny the very <u>next</u>
vacancy. She says this just to stop
Ginny from going on and on.

Toward the end of the conversation,
Mrs. Nichols comes into the kitchen.
The roomers leave. Mrs. Harris goes to
answer the doorbell and show prospective
tenants the vacancy.

Mrs. Nichols and Ginny talk in the
kitchen by themselves. Mrs. Nichols
asks Ginny to dispose of a wine bottle
for her -- and not tell her mother.
Through exposition, we learn that Mrs.
Nichols was feeling nostalgic last
night. She talks to Ginny about Joe,
her husband, and how they were in
summer stock together. There is a nice
rapport between Ginny and Mrs. Nichols.
Then the roomers start to intrude again.
The phone rings. Yetta gets it. It's
another person asking about the room.

Mrs. Harris comes into kitchen,
triumphantly. The room is rented.
Ginny's face reflects her disappointment. She wants it so desperately.
Her mother reminds her there's work to
do. Just before Ginny leaves the
kitchen, her mother tells her to take
her plant from the window sill. There's
no room for it. Ginny reaches for it,
not knowing where to put it. It is
displaced -- as she is.

                                        FADE OUT

FADE IN:

INT. LIVING ROOM -- AFTERNOON

Joan and Shirley are learning some new
dance steps -- phonograph is on -- and

as they dance, they accidentally turn
over the plant that is perched on a
small table. Ginny hears the clatter--
rescues the plant and brings it into
Room 2A.

INT. ROOM 2A -- DAY

This is Mrs. Nichols's room -- large,
more comfortable than any room in the
house. Ginny looks at it lovingly as
she makes the bed and straightens
things up.

Mrs. Nichols enters. They talk again.
Mrs. Nichols gets tearful as she talks
about her husband, Joe. She saw him
yesterday, she tells Ginny. Ginny is
shocked -- thought Mr. Nichols was
dead. It was just a story Mrs. Nichols
made up. She's always been in love
with him, but he liked the ladies too
much, and though he always pleaded to
come back to his wife after an affair,
she finally refused him. He left --
and (as she tells Ginny) she saw him
yesterday, quite by accident, in a
doorman's uniform at a posh hotel
near the beach. He was delighted to
see her and promised to call....As
they talk, the phone rings. Yetta
answers, calls to Mrs. Nichols. It's
for her.

Ginny finishes cleaning the room as she
overhears Mrs. Nichols talking lovingly
to Joe on the phone in the next room.
Mrs. Harris sees Ginny and is curious
about Ginny's delighted expression.

Ginny reminds her mother about the
promise -- the very next vacancy is hers.
Her mother says there won't be one for
years and years... Then, as Mrs. Nichols
finishes talking on the phone, she looks
at Ginny happily, and Ginny returns the
smile. Mrs. Harris wants to know what's
funny.

                              END OF ACT ONE

ACT TWO

INT. LIVING ROOM -- DAWN

Ginny is asleep on the living room
couch. At foot of couch is a carton
with all her possessions. The plant
peeps out of it. As the first rays of
light creep through the blinds, Ginny
opens her eyes. She sees Mrs. Nichols,
fully dressed, carrying packed bag.
Ginny calls to her, then follows her
into the kitchen.

INT. KITCHEN -- DAWN

Ginny gets some orange juice, offers
some to Mrs. Nichols, but she's too
nervous to have anything -- is waiting
for Mr. Nichols to call for her. They're
driving to Palm Springs -- belated
honeymoon. Ginny is happy for her.
They hear the car. She kisses Ginny
goodbye and leaves the house.

Ginny stands alone for a moment -- then
walks into the living room.

INT. LIVING ROOM -- DAWN

She looks at the hateful couch, rips
off the bedding, takes it and the
carton, and walks to the door of 2A.

INT. ROOM 2A -- MORNING

This is a precious moment. She is
moving into her own room. She stands
there, looking at the closed door --
her door ... Then she scurries around
rearranging things-- hangs prints on
the wall, puts plant on the sill,
unpacks books from the carton and
places them on night table. She tries
the bed -- pretends to be reading in
bed -- turns the table lamp on. She
is a child, glorying in the heady
feeling of having something of her own.
Suddenly, she is interrupted by her
mother.

Mrs. Harris thinks Ginny has gone out
of her mind. This is the best, the
largest room in the house. She can get
a very good price for it. Ginny can't
possibly have it. Ginny reminds her
of her promise to have the very "next"
vacancy. Mrs. Harris says she never
dreamed it would be this one. Ginny is
adamant. She pleads for it. Fights for
it. Mother hasn't time to argue with
her now -- leaves, very distraught.

                                    FADE OUT

FADE IN:

INT. LIVING ROOM -- EVENING

The boarders are there. Ginny is out.
Phone rings. Mrs. Harris can be heard,
answering it. It's a prospective tenant
asking about a room. Mrs. Harris is a
little vague. She doesn't want to turn
him away, but when Ginny enters, Mrs.
Harris cuts the conversation short.
She suggests the caller phone later.

Ginny is radiant. She found a typing
job and now she can pay for the room.
Mother doesn't like the news. She needs
Ginny to help in the house. Besides,
every bit of money should be going into
the bank for a "rainy day"... They are
interrupted by a boarder who says the
sink is stopped up again.

INT. ROOM 2A -- EVENING

Ginny enters, looks around her lovingly,
kicks off her shoes, and rests in the
easy chair. Knock on door -- Joan and
Shirley enter, wanting to borrow some
curlers. Ginny tells them about the
new job and the girls are happy for
her -- invite her to join them at the
Beach Casino. They know some nice guys.
The job calls for a celebration. Ginny
accepts.

                                   FADE OUT

FADE IN

INT. KITCHEN -- EVENING

Mrs. Harris is alone in the kitchen --
polishes silver. The phone rings. She
answers it. It's the same man asking
about a vacancy. Again, she hesitates,
but he offers a very good price. Mrs.
Harris says there's no harm in his
looking at the room. She hangs up,
very pleased. She looks at the clock.
It is 8:45.

                              DISSOLVE TO:

INT. LIVING ROOM -- NIGHT

The light from the foyer casts a shadow
on clock in living room. It is after
midnight. ... Girls enter from Beach
Casino date -- great spirits -- they
say goodnight to Ginny and go off to
their rooms.

Ginny stops in front of 2A. Puts key
in lock, tries to turn knob, but door
doesn't open. Key is stuck. She tries
again -- no luck. Starts to become
apprehensive -- then switches on lamp.
The light reveals couch made up as a
bed for her. Her hated carton holds all
her belongings. She can't believe it.
She's back where she started. Angry
tears. She flings herself across couch,
cries uncontrollably.

Mother hears Ginny's sobs and enters--
tries to console her. Ginny can't look
at her, but mother persists. She
points out she'll be getting <u>twice</u> the
money Ginny would pay -- and <u>that</u> money
will be hers (Ginny's) one day. It's
going into the bank... But this is no
consolation to Ginny. She pleads with
her mother to leave her alone! Mrs.
Harris slowly rises and walks away...
Hold on Ginny sobbing.

FADE OUT

FADE IN:

INT. KITCHEN -- MORNING

It is late morning. Mr. Miller, in
bathrobe, waits for his shower. Yetta
is eating french toast at the table.

Mrs. Harris enters -- says she almost
tripped on the suitcase in the foyer.
Wants to know whose it is. Yetta
doesn't know -- Shirley's? Joan's?
What about Ginny? No one has seen her
this morning... Mother walks toward the
living room as Ginny enters.

INT. LIVING ROOM -- MORNING

Ginny tells mother the suitcase is hers.
She's moving out. Ginny is quiet now,
controlled. Mother can't believe it.
Ginny explains it's something she must
do -- it didn't happen suddenly -- she's
thought about it for a long time. She's

put a deposit on a room in another rooming house in the area. Mother accuses
Ginny of hating her, but Ginny tries to
explain. They're two different people.
Ginny knows her needs. It's <u>more</u> than
money. She has to have a place of her
own -- a door she can close -- a
knowledge of who she is. Mother fights
back -- pleads -- but it's no use.
Ginny is afraid that she may "catch"
this frugality if she stays on. It's
like a disease, this preoccupation with
money, and she's afraid it will thwart
her if she stays. She knows she's
hurting her mother, but she can't help
it. It's a question of survival...
She kisses her quickly, takes the suitcase, and exits.

INT. NEW ROOM -- DAY

Hold on plant on windowsill -- then
pull back to show a neat, clean,
sparsely furnished room. It has
Ginny's personal touches -- the prints
on the wall -- her books, etc. Take
in Ginny who looks around the room
happily, then slowly closes the door,
leans against it, surveying her
"kingdom" as the credits roll.

XVI

THE SCRIPT

A Door You Can Close
by Michelle Cousin

THE FOLLOWING is the script in its entirety. It is divided into two acts in accordance with the producer's preference on this particular anthology show. (It was produced on a series called "Star Tonight" on the Mutual Network.)

Note the title page and the cast sheet that follow. This is standard form for all television manuscripts.

Note, too, that the play does not necessarily follow the breakdown to the letter. For example, in the breakdown I called for a kitchen scene in which Mrs. Harris is polishing silver. Then the phone rings in the living room and she walks to it.

In the actual play, I eliminated the kitchen scene. It seemed more expedient to start in the living room with the phone ringing and have Mrs. Harris walk into the frame.

Although a writer should follow the breakdown as closely as possible, a certain amount of flexibility is allowed, and it is permissible to make small changes.

A DOOR YOU CAN CLOSE

by Michelle Cousin

(an original half-hour television drama)

CAST

GINNY HARRIS   Nineteen -- more than
                       pretty. Sensitive,
                       intelligent with a
                       depth beyond her
                       years.

MRS. HARRIS   Ginny's mother.
                       Pinched face --
                       wiry body -- fru-
                       gal, authoritative.

MRS. NICHOLS   Middle-aged, blowsy,
                       good-hearted -- fad-
                       ed glamour.

THE ROOMERS

YETTA   Early twenties --
                       overweight -- good-
                       natured.

SHIRLEY   Middle twenties --
                       pretty

JOAN   Early twenties --
                       pleasant

HILDA HANES   Thirties -- whining
                       voice -- the com-
                       plainer

MR. MILLER   Forties -- set in
                       his ways -- non-
                       communicative

A DOOR YOU CAN CLOSE

FADE IN

1. EXT. PALM TREE -- DAY

    Hold on large printed sign tacked
    on tree. It reads: HOLLYWOOD
    ARMS -- ROOMS -- VACANCY.

                                    DISSOLVE TO:

2. INT. KITCHEN -- DAY

    This is a large, clean but worn
    community kitchen. Through the
    window can be seen the backyard or
    "patio," as the roomers call it.
    It boasts a palm tree and a clothes-
    line of wet bathing suits of the
    nineteen-fifty era.

    The California sun brightens the
    kitchen on this languid morning.
    The clock on the shelf above the
    sink says 10:30.

    The kitchen is cluttered with room-
    ers. JOAN and SHIRLEY, dressed in
    bathing suits, are peering into the
    refrigerator. They are both in their
    early twenties, pleasant, ordinary.

                        JOAN
            Nothing appeals to me.

                        SHIRLEY
            No wonder. You just ate.

MR. MILLER, a middle-aged man dressed in a faded bathrobe, stands outside the bathroom door, waiting his
turn. A towel is slung over his
shoulder. He holds a bar of soap.
Impatiently, he knocks on the bathroom door.

          MR. MILLER
    Come on, Miss Hanes, give
    somebody else a chance!

MRS. HARRIS enters, carrying fresh
linen. She is a frugal woman,
middle-aged, thin face, strong wiry
body.

          MRS. HARRIS
    There's a perfectly good
    shower upstairs, Mr.
    Miller.

          MR. MILLER
    Somebody'll get there
    before I do.

He exits to foyer.

    It always happens.

YETTA, a stout girl in shorts and
halter, enters. She carries her
wet bathing suit.

          MRS. HARRIS
    Now, Yetta, I told you,
    no wet bathing suits in-
    doors.

                    YETTA
        Gee whiz, Mrs. Harris—

                    MRS. HARRIS
        Those are the rules.
        You've got a perfect-
        ly good clothes-line
        in the back yard. That's
        what it's there for.

                    YETTA
        O.K. . . . O.K.

Starts out with the bathing suit.

        All the time, rules!

Mrs. Harris sees the girls at the
refrigerator.

                    MRS. HARRIS
        Girls, don't keep that door
        open forever!

Joan closes the door.

                    JOAN
        Come on, Shirl, let's fig-
        ure out what to wear to the
        dance tonight. I—

She stops as she sees GINNY who enters
with shopping bag in one hand and a
small plant wrapped in newspaper in
the other hand. Ginny is nineteen,
sensitive, intelligent.

        Hi, Ginny.

                    GINNY
            Hi.

                    SHIRLEY
            If you're going for a swim,
            maybe we'll join you later.

                    GINNY
            Yeah. . . O.K.

Joan and Shirley start to exit.
Ginny brings bundles to the table, as
she hears their exit lines.

                    JOAN
            I'm so sick of my white
            linen, I could die.

Shirley's voice fades as she follows
Joan out.

                    SHIRLEY
            Maybe if you cut out the
            sleeves...

Mrs. Harris turns to Ginny.

                    MRS. HARRIS
            Well, I was just about giv-
            ing you up.

                    GINNY
            The stores were crowded,
            Ma.

They start to unload the shopping
bag.

                    MRS. HARRIS
            Did you get everything?

                        GINNY
            Uh-huh. . .

Mrs. Harris points to plant wrapped
in newspaper.

                    MRS. HARRIS
            What's that?

                        GINNY
            A plant.

Ginny unwraps it and looks at it tend-
erly.

            It's pretty, isn't it, Ma?
            A little old lady was sell-
            ing it outside the market,
            and I couldn't resist—

                    MRS. HARRIS
            Always spending money
            foolishly!

                        GINNY

            It's not foolish. I want
            it! It's nice to have
            things growing.

                    MRS. HARRIS
            We got a palm tree in the
            backyard. It's enough for
            me. Never was for your

father, though. Till the
day he died—

        GINNY (cuts in)
Ma. . . Ma, there's some-
thing I want to ask you—

        MRS. HARRIS
Well, what is it?

        GINNY
It's about the room for
rent—

        MRS. HARRIS (cuts in)
Won't be for long. A
place near the beach don't
stay empty—

She stops as she sees MISS HANES
coming out of the bathroom.

        Did you have a nice show-
er, Miss Hanes?

Hilda Hanes is thirtyish, whiney
voice -- a spinster.

        MISS HANES
There's something wrong
with the hot water again.
Never works when you want
it to. Waits till you get
all soaped up and—

        MRS. HARRIS
I'll see what I can do
about it.

Miss Hanes talks as she exits to her
room.

>   MISS HANES
>   You can call the plumber,
>   that's what you can do.

Ginny waits till they're alone again,
then steels herself.

>   GINNY
>   (1) Ma. . . about that room.
>   I -- I'd like it myself!

>   MRS. HARRIS
>   3A?   That tiny old thing
>   on the top floor?

>   GINNY
>   It's not so small.   And
>   anyway, it doesn't matter
>   about the size.   Anything
>   would be better than sleep-
>   ing in the living room.

>   MRS. HARRIS
>   (2) That studio couch is prac-
>   tically brand new.   Cost me
>   a small fortune.   It's got
>   inner springs-

---

(1) This is the beginning of the conflict.

(2) When Mrs. Harris continues to oppose Ginny, the point of
attack has been established.

                    GINNY
          I don't care! I want a
          door I can close and a
          dresser and a closet. You
          don't know what it's like-

                    MRS. HARRIS
          I don't know! What kind
          of a "boodoir" do you
          think a front porch is?
          You don't hear me com-
          plaining.

                    GINNY
          That's not the point!

                    MRS. HARRIS
          The point is, if you took
          that room, we'd be losing
          that much rent every week.

                    GINNY
          But you won't! I'm not
          asking for it free. I'll
          pay.

                    MRS. HARRIS
          How?

                    GINNY
          I'll get a job. Why do
          you think I took typing
          at school?

                    MRS. HARRIS
          I need you here, Ginny.
          You know that. The place
          is too much for me to take
          care of.

                    GINNY
You can hire some help.

                    MRS. HARRIS
And pay wages? Where do
you think that'll come
from?

                    GINNY
Ma -- I'm trying to-

Yetta enters from backyard. She
crosses to foyer and talks as she
walks.

                    YETTA
I can't stay in that sun
another minute. I'm absolutely fried.

She exits.

                    MRS. HARRIS (to Ginny)
You're like your father was.
Good to look at, but you
don't know the first thing
about business.

                    GINNY
Maybe I don't, but I know
a little arithmetic.
You've got seven rooms
in this house, and every
one of them gives you a
pretty good rent. Even
with expenses, it seems
to me you'd have money
left over-

        MRS. HARRIS
And where do you think
that money's going, young
lady? Do you see me deck-
ed out like a movie star
with a shiny roadster
and a diamond tiara?

        GINNY
Oh, Ma, you know I don't
mean—

        MRS. HARRIS (cuts in)
I'll tell you where that
money is going! To you!
Every single cent of it!
So when I pass on, you'll
have something! . . . Not
like your father. He did-
n't leave one penny -- not
one single—

        GINNY
I don't want to hear about
that!

        MRS. HARRIS
Oh, don't you! . . . Now,
you listen to me, Miss
High-and-Mighty, some day
you're going to have what
I never had -- security.
You're not going to worry
about where your next
meal's coming from -- like
I did. You're going to—

        GINNY
"Going to" -- I'm sick of

those words. What about
<u>now</u>?

          MRS. HARRIS
Ginny—

          GINNY (cuts in)
Ever since I was this big,
I've wanted a room of my
own. Maybe it's not so
important to some people,
but it is to me! Just to
have a door I can close -
to feel <u>this is mine.</u>
<u>It belongs to me</u>!

She stops as she looks at her mother's
blank expression.

          That doesn't make sense
          to you, does it?

Miss Hanes enters from foyer.

          MISS HANES
Mrs. Harris, you said
you'd talk to Mr. Miller
about not playing his
radio so loud.

          MRS. HARRIS (resigned)
Yes, Miss Hanes. I will.

          MISS HANES
Well, I wish you'd do it
before I lose my hearing.

As she exits.

Some people don't know
the meaning of the word,
consideration. . .

Mrs. Harris sighs as she watches
Miss Hanes leave. Then she turns
to Ginny, putting an end to the
discussion.

            MRS. HARRIS
    Well, I'd better get back
    to my work. The linen
    needs changing.

            GINNY (earnestly)
    Would you just try, Ma?
    Would you let me have the
    room upstairs for a week --
    as an experiment?

            MRS. HARRIS
    The next one -- the very
    next one that comes up.

            GINNY
    But why not—

            MRS. HARRIS (sharply)
    For heaven's sake, Ginny,
    will you stop this—

She is interrupted as MRS. NICHOLS
approaches. Mrs. Nichols is a plump,
middle-aged woman with a vestige
of glamour. She pulls her marabou-
trimmed housecoat around her.

                    MRS. NICHOLS
          Morning. . .

                    MRS. HARRIS
          It's closer to noon,
          Mrs. Nichols.

                    MRS. NICHOLS
          Would you believe it,
          I don't even know the
          time. My watch stopped.

She smiles warmly at Ginny.

          Hello, Pumpkin.

                    GINNY
          Morning.

SOUND: The front door bell
rings.

                    MRS. HARRIS
          I'll get it. It's pro-
          bably about the room.

                    GINNY
          Ma -- couldn't you,
          please-

                    MRS. HARRIS
          The next one, Ginny.

She exits.

                    MRS. NICHOLS
          She's a hard worker,
          your ma.

                         GINNY
              Yes. . . she is.

                    MRS. NICHOLS
              Where'd you get the plant,
              honey?

                         GINNY (preoccupied)
              Hm-m . . . ? . . . Oh, it's
              mine. I bought it.

She places plant on window sill above
the sink.

              There's some coffee. Mrs.
              Nichols. Would you like a
              cup?

                    MRS. NICHOLS
              Later, thanks. . . What
              I really need is some
              bicarb. (she winks)
              Something I drank.

She reaches into housecoat pocket and
hands Ginny a bottle in a paper bag.

              You won't tell your ma,
              will you, hon, but I bought
              some wine and took it to
              my room last night.

                         GINNY
              I'll get rid of it for
              you.

Ginny puts it in the garbage pail.

Mrs. Nichols goes to the cupboard

to prepare the bicarbonate of
soda.

> MRS. NICHOLS
> You're a sweetie. . . I
> haven't touched a drop in
> ages, but last night -- I
> don't know -- the moon
> was so pretty -- I kept
> seeing it through my
> window -- and I got
> to thinking about a lot
> of things. Mr. Nichols,
> mostly. I was thinking
> of the time we were in
> summer stock. He couldn't
> act worth peanuts but
> there was something about
> him -- his smile -- I
> swear you could-

She stops as she sees Ginny's
preoccupied expression. She smiles
wryly.

> You haven't heard a word
> I said, have you, kid?

> GINNY
> Hm-m. . .? Oh, sure, sure
> I have.

Suddenly Ginny gets water for the
plant.

> MRS. NICHOLS
> What's the matter? You
> want to tell me about it?

SOUND: Phone rings from the living
room. Mrs. Nichols looks hopeful.

          I wonder if that's for me.

3.   INT. LIVING ROOM - DAY

This is a well-worn living room,
sparsely furnished with a studio
couch, two armchairs, a few end
tables, lamps, and a worn but
clean carpet. On one wall adjacent
to the foyer, hangs a pay telephone.

The phone is ringing as Yetta enters
and calls out.

                    YETTA
          I'll get it. (in phone)
          Hello. . .Who? This is
          Yetta. (louder) Yetta!...
          What number do you want?

Mrs. Harris enters from the foyer.
Yetta is shouting into the phone.

          No! This is not the laun-
          dry!

                  MRS. HARRIS
          Not so loud, Yetta.

Mrs. Harris exits to kitchen.

Yetta hangs up.

                    YETTA
          Rules! All the time,
          rules!

4. INT. KITCHEN - DAY

    Mrs. Nichols and Ginny are at the
    kitchen table.

    Mrs. Harris enters, pleased.

                MRS. HARRIS
        Well, the room's taken.

                GINNY
        For sure?

                MRS. HARRIS
        All moved in. Bag and
        baggage. Plus two weeks'
        rent in advance.

    Ginny looks unhappy but Mrs. Harris
    ignores the look.

        That's the way I like it.
        One hundred per cent full
        up!

    Ginny doesn't respond to her mother's
    elation. Mrs. Nichols senses the
    tension and tries to ease it.

                MRS. NICHOLS
        Anybody join me in coffee?

    She begins to heat coffee.

                MRS. HARRIS
        We've got work to do,
        haven't we, Ginny? The
        linen needs changing.

>   I'll take the top floor.
>   You start down here.
>
>   GINNY
>   Yes, Ma. . .

Ginny starts to exit but Mrs. Harris
stops her as she sees the plant on
the window sill.

>   MRS. HARRIS
>   Wait a minute. You forgot
>   this. Hate things clutter-
>   ing up the place.

Ginny holds the plant carefully.

>   MRS. NICHOLS
>   Where you going to put it,
>   Ginny?
>
>   GINNY
>   I don't know, Mrs. Nichols. . .
>   I don't know.

>   FADE OUT

FADE IN:

5.   INT. LIVING ROOM - DAY

We hold on a small, old-fashioned
phonograph. A dance record of the
fifties is playing. Pull back to
show Joan and Shirley practising
the dance steps.

                    JOAN
          Come on, Shirl, you're
          not getting the beat.

                    SHIRLEY
          Give me time. I'm
          just learning.

We pull back farther to see Ginny's
plant perched on a small table not
too far from the girls.

Miss Hanes comes into the room holding
a book. She looks annoyed.

                    MISS HANES
          If it's not Mr. Miller's
          radio, it's this noise-
          maker here!

                    JOAN
          Why don't you try wearing
          ear plugs, Miss Hanes?

Miss Hanes exits to kitchen.

                    MISS HANES (as she exits)
          I'll probably have to, to
          keep my sanity.

Joan snickers after Miss Hanes leaves
the room.

                    JOAN
          What sanity?

                    SHIRLEY
          Look, just because she's
          a square—

                    JOAN
Are we practising or aren't
we?

                 SHIRLEY
O.K. O.K.

They pause to get the beat. As they
dance, Shirley does a fast twirl and
accidentally knocks over the plant.

                    JOAN
Look out!

The plant falls to the floor.

Gee, you're clumsy.

Joan turns off the record.

Ginny opens the door of room 2A,
which leads into the living room.
Over her skirt, she wears an apron.
She stoops to pick up the plant.

                 SHIRLEY
I didn't even see it. Who
put it on the table in the
first place?

              GINNY (shaky)
I did. . . It's mine.

                 SHIRLEY
Gee, I'm sorry, Gin. . . I
didn't even see it.

                  GINNY
It's. . . all right.

She tries to doctor the plant.

Joan and Shirley look at Ginny as
she scans the room for another place
to put the plant. Finally she crosses
to room 2A, carries the plant in with
her, and closes the door.

6.   INT. ROOM 2A - DAY

The room reflects its owner, Mrs.
Nichols. As Ginny walks to the small
table near the window, we take in
articles on dresser: jewelry box
spilling over with cheap costume
jewelry -- assorted perfume -- a
music box, and a photograph of Joe
Nichols taken years ago. Clothes
are strewn on chairs. There are
movie magazines scattered around
the room.

Ginny goes back to her bed-making
after placing the plant on the table.
She tries to conceal angry tears with
a grim determination to finish her
work. Occasionally she pauses and
looks about her, longingly.

Mrs. Nichols opens the door and
enters.

                    MRS. NICHOLS
          Hi. . .

                    GINNY
          I'm almost through here,
          Mrs. Nichols.

                    MRS. NICHOLS
           It's O.K. Pumpkin. Don't
           hurry.

She pauses at mirror over dresser -
looks at her reflection -- then at
Joe's picture. She is lost in thought
and suddenly realizes Ginny is staring
at her.

           Did I ever show you this?

She winds the music-box.

                Joe gave it to me the first
                year we were married.

It begins to play softly. Mrs.
Nichols becomes nostalgic.

                It's crazy, isn't it? I
                mean how you can get attach-
                ed to something like this.
                After all these years,
                you'd think-

She chokes up and puts her hand
to her face.

Ginny looks concerned.

                    GINNY
           Mrs. Nichols-

                    MRS. NICHOLS
           Don't mind me, baby. I'm
           just not feeling so good,

that's all. I don't know
what's the matter with me.
Yes, I do. It was seeing
Joe again. That's what
started me off.

                GINNY
You mean you -- you dreamt
about him last night?

                MRS. NICHOLS
I <u>saw</u> him, baby. In person.

                GINNY
But I thought he was de---

She can't say "dead."

I mean all the time when
you said you lost him --

                MRS. NICHOLS
Sure I lost him. I lost
him to another woman. A
couple, if you want to
know the truth. Oh, he
got tired of them soon --
but I wouldn't take him
back. Not me! I was
going to be a great star
and he'd come crawling
like they do in the movies.
Only it didn't work that
way. He left-- and I ended up-

She doesn't trust her voice.

                          GINNY
            . . . But you saw him
            again?

                     MRS. NICHOLS
            Yeah. . . just by accident,
            see? I was coming out of
            work and I passed that new
            swanky hotel near the
            beach -- and there he was --
            standing there in his door-
            man's uniform like he owned
            the joint. I tell you I
            got so shaky, I -- I-

    She stops and listens.

            Was that the phone?

                          GINNY
            I didn't hear anything...
            Did he say he'd call?

                     MRS. NICHOLS
            Yeah. . . but I think he
            was trying to make me
            feel good. . . You want
            to hear a laugh, kid?
            I'd go with him any-
            where. All he's got
            to do is ask me. That's
            pride for you, huh? I'd
            give up this place so
            fast-

    SOUND: The phone rings off.

Mrs. Nichols freezes.

> GINNY
> Maybe that's him.

> MRS. NICHOLS
> Are you kidding? It's
> for one of the girls.

The phone stops ringing.

Mrs. Nichols walks to the dresser.

> Well, I'd better think of
> getting dressed. Maybe I'll
> take in a movie today. There's
> a good one playing-

She is interrupted by a knock on
the door.

> YETTA (off)
> Mrs. Nichols, telephone.

Mrs. Nichols opens the door.

> MRS. NICHOLS
> For me. . . ?

> YETTA
> Yeah. . . It's a man.

Mrs. Nichols looks at Ginny who smiles
encouragingly.

> MRS. NICHOLS
> Thanks, Yetta.

Yetta exits to her own room.

           YETTA
     All I ever get is wrong
     numbers.

7.   INT. LIVING ROOM - DAY

Mrs. Nichols crosses to the phone.
The living room is empty at the
moment and Mrs. Nichols enjoys the
rare privacy as she picks up the
receiver.

          MRS. NICHOLS (in phone)
     Hello. . . Joe, it's great
     to hear your voice. . .
     sure. I'm fine. . . to-
     night?

Mrs. Harris enters, carrying
"VACANCY" sign. She ignores Mrs.
Nichols at phone -- looks around
for Ginny -- then calls.

          MRS. HARRIS
     Ginny. . .

Ginny comes out of Mrs. Nichols'
room.

          GINNY
     I'm almost finished in
     there, Ma.

          MRS. HARRIS
     Good. . .

                MRS. NICHOLS (in phone)
        Sure I can make it. . .
        what time?

                MRS. HARRIS (to Ginny)
        Thank goodness we can put
        this away.

She refers to the sign.

                MRS. NICHOLS (in phone)
        Do you, Joe. . Are you?

                MRS. HARRIS (to Ginny)
        The furniture in here
        needs dusting.

                MRS. NICHOLS (in phone)
        Sure I'm listening, Joe. . .

                GINNY
        Ma. . . you <u>did</u> say I get
        the very next room, didn't
        you?

                MRS. HARRIS
        Now, Ginny, don't start
        that again.

                MRS. NICHOLS (in phone)
        Oh, Joe, you don't know
        how much that means to me. .

                GINNY
        You did promise, Ma.

                MRS. HARRIS
        Nobody's moving out, Ginny.

        MRS. NICHOLS (in phone)
I will, Joe. . .

        MRS. HARRIS
It may take years before
there's another vacancy.
If you listen to-

She stops as she sees Ginny's con-
fident smile. Mrs. Nichols has hung
up the receiver and stands looking
at Ginny -- a secret, happy smile
is exchanged between them.

Mrs. Harris looks puzzled.

      (to Ginny) What are you
      grinning like that for?

        GINNY
Am I, Ma? . . .

She continues to look at Mrs.
Nichols.

      I didn't know I was.

                  FADE OUT

END OF ACT ONE

ACT TWO

FADE IN:

8.   INT. LIVING ROOM - NIGHT

Ginny is asleep on the studio couch in
the living room. Her bathrobe is on
a chair nearby. At the foot of the
couch is a carton which contains books,
a few prints (Degas, Renoir), a pad
and pencil, and the plant. These
are Ginny's "belongings."

As we pull back, the first rays of
morning light are beginning to peep
through the blinds.

Ginny opens her eyes to see Mrs.
Nichols, fully dressed, coming out
of her room. She carries an overnight bag. She heads for the kitchen
but stops as she hears Ginny's voice.

             GINNY (softly)
        Mrs. Nichols, what time
        is it?

             MRS. NICHOLS
        Five-thirty...go back
        to sleep, honey.

             GINNY
        I'll be getting up soon,
        anyway.

She reaches for her robe.

When's Joe calling for
you?

                    MRS. NICHOLS
          In a couple of minutes.
          We want to get an early
          start before the traf-
          fic gets bad.

                    GINNY
          They say it's a beau-
          tiful drive to Palm
          Springs.

                    MRS. NICHOLS
          Ever been there?

                    GINNY
          No, never.

                    MRS. NICHOLS
          Me neither.

There is a pause.

          Crazy, isn't it?
          After twenty years
          I'm finally going on
          a honeymoon. We never
          had one, you know.
          Couldn't afford it.

Ginny senses Mrs. Nichols' tension.

                    GINNY
          Would you like some
          orange juice?

                    MRS. NICHOLS
No thanks, baby, I'll
get some on the road.

She looks at her watch.

          I wonder what's keeping
          him?

                    GINNY
He'll be here.

                    MRS. NICHOLS
...Do I look O.K.?

                    GINNY
You look fine.

                    MRS. NICHOLS
I don't feel so fine,
I can tell you. I'm
as nervous as a young
bride...Look, Pumpkin, .
you don't have to wait
with me. Go on back
to bed.

                    GINNY
But I'm usually up at
this hour. It's my
favorite time...It's
so quiet.

                    MRS. NICHOLS
It's kind of spooky
to me...but then, no-
thing seems real any-
way. You take Joe and

me. I can't believe
it yet--the way it all
happened. Like a
miracle.

Ginny listens attentively.

Just last week, I was
sitting here telling
you about him--re-
member?

          GINNY
I remember.

          MRS. NICHOLS
Then a phone call--
a couple of dates--
and here I am-

SOUND: Approaching car in driveway.

It's Joe!

SOUND: The car comes to a stop. Mrs.
Nichols puts light coat on.

          MRS. NICHOLS
Say good-bye to your
ma for me, will you
honey? I tried to yes-
terday but she looked
so sore when Joe came
for my things-

They walk to the front door.

                    GINNY
          She's not mad at you.
          Ma just doesn't like
          change, that's all.
          And you've been here
          so long-

SOUND: A light horn of the car. off.

             MRS. NICHOLS
          I'd better run...

She kisses Ginny's cheek.

             Good-bye, Pumpkin.
             I'll call you soon's
             we get back, and you'll
             come to dinner, O.K.?

                    GINNY
             Sure.

Mrs. Nichols exits.   Ginny waves.

             Bye...

Ginny closes the front door.   Then,
her triumphant smile tells us she is
now the owner of the new vacancy.
The morning sun bursts full on Ginny's
face as she stands, smiling to herself.

Now she goes into action.   She takes
the carton at the foot of the couch
and heads towards room 2A.

9.   INT. ROOM 2A - MORNING

    She enters and closes the door. This
    is a precious moment to her. She
    leans against the door, enjoying the
    wonder of having a room of her own--
    a door she can close. For a moment,
    she doesn't know where to start.

    Suddenly she bursts into activity.
    She opens the closet, looks at her-
    self in the full-length mirror; walks
    to the dresser--opens a few of the
    drawers. She unpacks the books from
    the carton, puts them on the night
    table. She tries the bed for size
    and pretends to be reading in bed.
    She turns the bed lamp on.

    She finds a perfect spot for her plant
    on the small, round table next to the
    window. And on the opposite wall, she
    sees a new home for the two prints
    which she quickly hangs on the nails
    already there. In the midst of her
    excitement, there is a knock on the
    door.

                MRS. HARRIS
          Mrs. Nichols...?

    A pause. She knocks again.

          Mrs. Nichols-

    Ginny opens the door.

                    GINNY
          She's gone, Ma. She
          told me to tell you
          good-bye.

                  MRS. HARRIS
          What are <u>you</u> doing
          here?

                    GINNY
          Arranging my room...
          Oh, Ma, I've got so
          many wonderful ideas.
          I'm going to make a
          dressing-table with a
          little skirt--you
          know?...and I'm going
          to rearrange these
          chairs--and I'm going
          to get a headboard--
          and in my closet, I'm-

     She stops as she sees her mother's
     grim, unbelieving expression.

          What's the matter, Ma?

                  MRS. HARRIS
          Have you gone right
          out of your mind!

                    GINNY
          No...Just because I
          want to make a few
          changes...I'm not going
          to hurt anything. I
          just want it to be
          part of me, that's all.

When you live in a
room-

She looks at her mother again, this
time apprehensively.

I...<u>am</u> going to live
in it, Ma?

          MRS. HARRIS
Listen to me, Ginny-

          GINNY
You said so. You said
so yourself. When I
asked for 3A. You
said the <u>very next</u>
<u>one</u>. Remember?

          MRS. HARRIS
Yes, I remember. But
listen to me-

          GINNY
Well, this is it. The
very next one.

          MRS. HARRIS
Ginny-

          GINNY
It's mine! You pro-
mised it to me!

          MRS. HARRIS
Will you stop saying
that!

            GINNY
But it's true. You
can't go back on your
word now.

            MRS. HARRIS
I didn't say I would..
I just want to point
out a few things,
that's all. This hap-
pens to be the best
room in the house.
It's bigger, brighter,
has more furniture-

            GINNY
I know that, Ma-

            MRS. HARRIS
Mrs. Nichols never paid
me what it's worth.
But she'd been here
so long-

            GINNY
I'll pay you. I'll
get a job. You'll see.

            MRS. HARRIS
I need you here, Gin-
ny. I need you to
help me.

            GINNY
We'll get help. We'll
manage, Ma.

                    MRS. HARRIS
You don't understand.

                       GINNY
I understand <u>this</u>.
All my life I've waited
to have a room of my
own. It's the one
thing I want! I'd
have been satisfied
with a <u>little</u> room--
I pleaded for 3A, but
no, you had to find
some excuse-

                    MRS. HARRIS
Ginny, please-

                    GINNY
There're no more ex-
cuses, Ma. You pro-
mised this to me! And
now I've got it! I'm
not going to give it
up! You can't ask me
to!

                    MRS. HARRIS
You're stubborn, like
your father was. Once
he got a bug in his
head, there was no
changing him.

                    GINNY
There's no changing me
either, Ma.

A pause. Mrs. Harris is momentarily
blocked.

>   MRS. HARRIS
>   I'll go start break-
>   fast.

Mrs. Harris turns and walks to the
door. Ginny watches her. Then softly
she says:

>   GINNY
>   Ma...

>   MRS. HARRIS
>   And turn the light
>   out! It costs money!

Mrs. Harris exits.

Ginny stands against the door, hurt
and angry. She stares at the lamp
without making a move to turn the
light out. We hold on the light.

>   FADE OUT

10.   INT. LIVING ROOM - NIGHT

Mr. Miller is in the easy chair near
the window. He is reading the paper
as he smokes a cigar.

Joan and Shirley enter from foyer.
They are returning from work and are
in the midst of a conversation.

                    JOAN
          ..so then he says to
          me, "Listen, I'm really
          a talent scout, see?"

                  SHIRLEY
          What did you say,
          "Isn't everybody?"

                    JOAN
          Wait till I tell you-

She sees Mr. Miller.

          Oh, hi, Mr. Miller.

              MR. MILLER
          Evening, girls.

Hilda Hanes rushes into the room from
the kitchen. She looks upset. She
is wearing an apron over her house-
dress.

                MISS HANES
          I can't find my but-
          ter. It was on the
          top shelf in the re-
          frigerator...Mr. Mil-
          ler-.

               MR. MILLER
          Naturally, just by
          looking at me, you can
          tell I'm the type who
          takes things.

                    MISS HANES
          You needn't be sar-
          castic.

Joan nudges Shirley to leave. The
girls exit to their room.

SOUND: The telephone rings.

Miss Hanes ignores the girls and continues to speak to Mr. Miller.

               I was only asking a
               simple question.

Yetta leaps into the room to answer
the phone.

                    YETTA
          I'll get it!

Miss Hanes exits to the kitchen, luck-
ily avoiding a "collision" with Yetta.

               (in phone) Hello...Yes,

               this is the Hollywood
               Arms. This is--...No.
               No, I'm not the owner.

Mrs. Harris comes down the steps as
Yetta keeps talking.

               About a room? No,
               we're all filled up-

                    MRS. HARRIS
          I'll take it, Yetta.

                    YETTA
          But, Mrs. Harris-

Mr. Miller, exasperated, folds his
paper and exits to his room.

               MRS. HARRIS
          I'll take it.

She means business. Yetta relin-
quishes the phone. Mrs. Harris, as
she takes the receiver, sounds busi-
nesslike.

               (in phone) Hello, this
          is Mrs. Harris...the
          owner.

Yetta exits.

               Well, we did have a
          vacancy a couple of
          weeks ago...Just your-
          self, are you? uh-huh...
          Well, it is and it
          isn't at the moment.
          What'd you say the
          name was? Foster?
          Yes, Mr. Foster...Fine.
          Bye.

She hangs up. Looks at Ginny who is
waiting to talk to her.

               You look all worn out.

                    GINNY
          I'm not. I've got
          something to tell you.

                    MRS. HARRIS
          I know. Job-hunting's
          no picnic.

                    GINNY
          I'm not going job-hun-
          ting any more.

                    MRS. HARRIS
          Well, I thought you'd
          come to your senses-

                    GINNY
          I've got a job!

                    MRS. HARRIS
          You what!

                    GINNY
          I know it seems impos-
          sible my first day
          out--but it's true.
          They gave me a typing
          test, and I was so
          nervous, I didn't
          think I could make it,
          but I did. And I
          start tomorrow and the
          hours--

          Stops talking and is conscious of her
          mother's disapproval.

          I thought you'd be
          pleased.

                    MRS. HARRIS
          I liked things like

they were. You had a
job here, helping me.

                    GINNY
But Ma--

                    MRS. HARRIS

And a good chance to
save money. But now
there'll be carfare
and lunches and I don't
know what-all.

                    GINNY
There'll be enough to
pay for my room. I
figured it out. Five
dollars more than Mrs.
Nichols paid you.

                    MRS. HARRIS
That money belongs in
a bank. That's where.
For a rainy day-

                    GINNY
Please, Ma--

                    MRS. HARRIS
But you're like your
father was. High-
falutin' ideas-

Miss Hanes comes in from the kitchen.

                    MISS HANES
Mrs. Harris, the sink's

stopped up again.
That's the third time
this week--

      MRS. HARRIS
I'll fix it, Miss
Hanes. Don't you wor-
ry.

She exits with Miss Hanes to the
kitchen.

      Needs a little pumping,
      that's all.

Ginny looks after her mother and Miss
Hanes with a resigned expression.
Then she starts for her own room.

11. INT ROOM 2A - NIGHT

Ginny smiles as she enters the room.
The "little touches" reflect Ginny's
personality. It is a charming room--
livable--orderly.

She pours some water from a pitcher
into a glass and waters her plant.

SOUND: Knock on the door.

      GINNY
...Yes?

      JOAN (off)
It's us.

Ginny opens the door to Joan and
Shirley who are in bathrobes.

            GINNY
        Oh, hi.

            JOAN
        Got any extra bobby-pins,
        Ginny? We're all out.

            GINNY
        Sure. Come in.

The girls enter and are shocked at the
"magnificence" of the room.

            SHIRLEY
        Hey, will you look at
        this place!

            JOAN
        It's the Waldorf.

            GINNY
        Glad you like it.

She gets the bobby-pins.

        I love it!...

She hands them the pins.

        Here you are.

            JOAN
        Thanks. We'll give
        them back tomorrow.

                    GINNY
          Don't bother.   It's a
          present.

                    JOAN
          Hey, thanks.

                    GINNY
          To celebrate my new
          job.

                    SHIRLEY
          You got a job?

                    JOAN
          No kidding!

                    GINNY
          Today!   I still can't
          believe it!

                    SHIRLEY
          This calls for a cele-
          bration.

                    JOAN
          Hey, we're going dan-
          cing at the Beach
          Casino tonight.   Why
          don't you join us?

                    GINNY
          Thanks, but I haven't
          got a date.

                    JOAN
          Listen, my date knows
          every guy on the stag-

                    line. You'll be
                    mobbed.

                         SHIRLEY
                    What'd you say?

                         GINNY
                    ...I don't think so.

                         JOAN
                    They're nice guys.

                         SHIRLEY
                    You'll like them..

                         JOAN
                    Live a little.

          Ginny pauses, then makes up her mind.

                         GINNY
                    O.K...O.K. I will!

          The girls smile back at her.

                              FADE OUT

          FADE IN

12.   INT. LIVING ROOM - NIGHT

          One small lamp is burning in the living
          room. It illuminates the clock which
          says 8:30. It is one of those rare
          moments when no-one is in the room.
          We hear the ticking of the clock.
          Then.

SOUND: Telephone rings.

Mrs. Harris comes in from the kitchen.
She looks a bit weary as she reaches
for the phone.

> MRS. HARRIS (in phone)
> Hello...yes, this is
> Mrs. Harris. Who..?
> Oh, you called a couple
> of hours ago, didn't
> you? Uh-huh...Well, I
> tell you, Mr. Foster,
> it's not exactly a va-
> cancy-

She stops and listens and her face
reacts happily.

> Well, that is a good
> fair price, I should
> say--but you see, it's
> not exactly--Hmm? No,
> no harm in looking at
> it. Guess that could
> be arranged...Yes, I'll
> be here all evening,
> but I can't guarantee--
> well, since you put it
> that way...I under-
> stand...uh-huh. Just
> looking...See you, Mr.
> Foster...Good-bye.

She hangs up, looking very pleased.

FADE OUT

```
        FADE IN:

13.     INT. LIVING ROOM - NIGHT

        Since the lamp-light is off, we can
        barely distinguish the face of the
        clock.  The light from the foyer
        casts a shadow into the living room;
        except for the ticking of the clock,
        everything is still.

        Joan, Shirley, and Ginny enter the
        foyer from the front door.  They have
        obviously had an enjoyable evening--
        and are in good, if muted spirits.
        They talk softly as they enter the
        living room.

                    JOAN
              How do you like that
              girl!

        She refers to Ginny.

              She goes with no date,
              and three guys fight
              to take her home.

                    SHIRLEY
              I didn't know you
              could dance like that.

                    GINNY
              I can't, really...it
              was just that I...I
              was feeling so good-
```

                    JOAN
          We won't be feeling so
          good when that alarm
          goes off in the mor-
          ning.

                    SHIRLEY
          To bed, "working
          girls"!

                    GINNY
          And that includes me...

Joan and Shirley start for their room.

                    JOAN & SHIRLEY
          Night, Ginny...

Ginny starts towards her room.

                    GINNY
          Night--and thanks.

The girls exit.

Ginny gets her key and tries to turn
the lock. It doesn't budge. She
tries again, but it is impossible to
open the door. She switches on the
lamp--feels a little panicky--but
again makes an effort to open the
door. Frustrated, unbelieving, she
turns and sees the studio couch made
up into a bed and the hateful carton
with all her belongings at the foot
of the couch.

(3) Slowly, Ginny walks back to the couch—
dazed, hurt. Angry tears well up.
She falls across the couch, burying
her face in her hands and sobbing uncontrollably.

Mrs. Harris, in slippers and bathrobe,
rushes to Ginny's side. Her voice is
placating.

                    MRS. HARRIS
          Ginny...Ginny, listen
          to me.

                    GINNY (through tears)
          Go away! Just go
          away!

                    MRS. HARRIS
          I didn't want to rent
          it. But this Mr. Fos-
          ter--he kept calling--
          said he just wanted to
          look at the room-

                    GINNY
          Why didn't you tell
          him it was taken?

                    MRS. HARRIS
          I did. I told him.
          But the minute he saw

-----

(3) This is the beginning of the crisis — the emotional outburst
    that cannot be controlled. It is the turning point of the play.

it, he kept pestering
me till I had to say
"yes."

          GINNY
How could you, Ma? It
was mine. Didn't you
think of me at all?

          MRS. HARRIS
Oh, you little fool,
who else was I thinking
of! Listen, you don't
know the whole story.
He's paying me twice
the rent! Twice, mind
you. And where do you
think that extra money's
going! Right straight to
you, Ginny! I'm going to
open your very own bank
account in the morning!
Why, in a couple of years-

          GINNY (cuts in)
I don't care about a couple
of years! I'll be dead by
then!

          MRS. HARRIS
Don't talk like that!

          GINNY
Why did you do it, Ma? I
loved that room! I wanted it
so! Why did you—

She stops as a fresh burst of tears choke
the words.

Mrs. Harris looks bewildered. She tries
to be tender -- touches Ginny's head
lightly. Ginny bristles.

Go away! Don't touch me!

                    MRS. HARRIS
          Ginny-

                    GINNY
          Leave me alone!

Mrs. Harris slowly rises and walks
away. Ginny continues to sob.

                              FADE OUT

FADE IN

14.   INT.   KITCHEN - DAY

Mr. Miller, in bathrobe, is waiting
outside the bathroom.

Yetta is eating french toast at the
kitchen table and looking at the
Sunday paper.

                    YETTA
          Would you like some french
          toast while you're waiting,
          Mr. Miller?

                    MR. MILLER
          Thanks, I ate already.

                    YETTA
          So did I! But that's

                    no reason to stop. On
                    Sunday a person should
                    eat as much as-

Mrs. Harris enters from living room.

          Oh, hi, Mrs. Harris.

                    MRS. HARRIS
          Morning...which of you's
          going somewhere?

                    MR. MILLER
          Me?...I'm going to take
          a shower if this door
          ever-

                    MRS. HARRIS (cuts in)
          I mean travelling.
          There's a suitcase in
          the foyer. Whose is
          it?

                    YETTA
          Search me...did you ask
          the girls?

                    MRS. HARRIS
          They're not up yet.

SOUND: Front door opens and closes.

Mrs. Harris calls out.

          That you, Ginny?

15.   INT. LIVING ROOM - DAY

Ginny enters. She is self-composed,
completely over the hysteria of
the previous night.

Mrs. Harris enters from kitchen.

          MRS. HARRIS
     Well, where've you been?
     To the beach?

          GINNY
     No, Ma...not this morning.

Mrs. Harris senses a tension. She
changes the subject.

          MRS. HARRIS
     You must be hungry. Why
     don't I-

          GINNY (cuts in)
     No, don't bother, please.
     (pause) Ma, I've got some-
     thing to tell you.

          MRS. HARRIS
     ...That fool suitcase in
     the middle of the floor.
     Someone's going to-

          GINNY
     It's mine. That is, I
     borrowed it from Shirley.

          MRS. HARRIS
     ...What for, Ginny?

                    GINNY (evenly)
    (4) I'm going away, Ma.

                    MRS. HARRIS
    You mean on a trip...

                    GINNY
    No. I'm going away for
    good.

Mrs. Harris stares at her.

    I'm moving out!

                    MRS. HARRIS
    You're joking...It's
    one of your jokes.
    You're trying to fool
    me!

                    GINNY
    No, I'm not, Ma. I'm
    just doing what I have
    to do, that's all.

                    MRS. HARRIS
    Leaving home! Leaving
    me! This is something
    you have to do-

_____

(4) This is the beginning of the climax. Ginny, composed now,
    has reasoned a solution to her problem. This is the highest
    point of the play in terms of what her actions mean to
    herself and to her mother.

                    GINNY
Yes, Ma...It didn't hap-
pen all of a sudden.
I've thought about it
a long time.

               MRS. HARRIS
And where will you go,
may I ask?

                    GINNY
I found a place. Only
five blocks away. It's
a new rooming house. I
paid a deposit.

               MRS. HARRIS
You're getting back at
me, aren't you? For
renting your room!

                    GINNY
No, Ma--I'm not-

          MRS. HARRIS (cuts in)
You hate me! Why don't
you say it?

                    GINNY
I don't. Honestly, Ma.
I thought I did for a
while and it scared me--
...but I know now -- (stops)
Look, we're too different
people. We don't see things
the same way.

                    MRS. HARRIS
        It's 'cause you're young.
        In a couple of years
        you'll know I'm right.
        When you have your own
        money-

                    GINNY
        Money! That's all you
        care about!

                    MRS. HARRIS
        For you, Ginny! It's
        all for you! I want
        you to have things!

                    GINNY
        What things? What can
        you give me?

                    MRS. HARRIS
        Not now. But in five or
        ten years...

                    GINNY
        "On a rainy day."

                    MRS. HARRIS
        Yes! Don't make fun of
        that saying! It's a
        good one! You have
        to save up for a rainy
        day!

                    GINNY
        Ma, would you like to
        know something? It's

pouring outside!   It's
been pouring for-

    MRS. HARRIS (cuts in)
I don't know what you're
talking about!

      GINNY (earnestly)
There are some things
you can't save for, Ma--
like--like just knowing
you're alive--and being
glad of it! And--and--
knowing who you are--
and--having a door you
can close-

    MRS. HARRIS
Ginny, listen-

      GINNY
It's a kind of feeling
inside--I don't know the
word--"dignity," may-
be...I can't put that
in the bank, Ma. I
need it now!

    MRS. HARRIS
I can't let you go!
Give yourself time!

      GINNY
There is no time!
Don't you see, Ma, I'm
afraid to stay here--
afraid I'll shrivel up
inside. Whatever this

money business is, I
don't want to catch it.

          MRS. HARRIS
You make it sound like
a disease.

          GINNY
Maybe it is, in a way.
(pause) When I was
packing this morning,
I found a Mother's Day
gift--the one I gave
you three years ago.
It was never even taken
out of its box.

          MRS. HARRIS
I'll use it some day.

          GINNY
Will you, Ma...?

     MRS. HARRIS (desperately)
Ginny, I never had anything!
Never! Your father-

          GINNY
I know. Pop was a dreamer.
Who knows, he might have
been something more if --
(stops) Funny...I always
think of him as a pretty
rich man...(pause) I have
to go now.

She walks toward her suitcase.

                          MRS. HARRIS
                    Ginny -- please don't-

                            GINNY
                    We'll be neighbors, Ma.
                    I'll come and see you.
                    We'll be friends.

She kisses her mother on the cheek.
Then, with her suitcase, exits quickly.

                          MRS. HARRIS
                    Ginny!

She stands stunned, looking after her.

                                    DISSOLVE TO:

16.   INT. NEW ROOM - DAY

We hold on Ginny's plant on the window
sill. Then we pull back to show a neat,
sparsely furnished room. Ginny's prints
are on the wall, her books on the night
table. Finally, we take in Ginny who
leans against the closed door of her
room, happily surveying her kingdom.

CREDITS ROLL

                    THE END